KU-367-891

one hundred
Wisdom Stories
from around the world

one hundred
Wisdom Stories
from around the world

compiled by

MARGARET SILF

LION

Copyright in the collection © 2003 Margaret Silf

Margaret Silf asserts the moral right
to be identified as the compiler of this work

Published by
Lion Publishing plc
Wilkinson House, Jordan Hill Road,
Oxford OX2 8DR, England
www.lion-publishing.co.uk
ISBN 978 0 7459 5541 4

First edition 2003
This edition 2011
10 9 8 7 6 5 4 3 2 1 0

All rights reserved

Distributed by
UK: Marston Book Services, PO Box 269, Abingdon, Oxon, OX14 4YN
USA: Trafalgar Square Publishing, 814 N. Franklin Street, Chicago, IL 60610
USA Christian Market: Kregel Publications, PO Box 2607, Grand Rapids, MI 49501

Acknowledgments
Cover & inside images: textured background © Jussi Santaniemi/iStockphoto; main image
© Ka Ho Leung/iStockphoto

A catalogue record for this book is available
from the British Library

Typeset in 11/14 Baskerville

Printed and bound in the UK by MPG Books Ltd.

Contents

Introduction

For as long as human beings have pondered the meaning of their own lives and of the world they live in, it has been through storytelling that much of this exploration has happened. In stories, the natural human delight in narrative walks hand in hand with the equally powerful desire within us to make sense of ourselves.

The world abounds in 'wisdom stories'. Some of these stories suggest explanations for who we are and how we came to be who we are. Others offer guidance on how to live, how to relate to each other and how to cope with life's joys and crises. Almost all of them can be engaged with at different levels – from the simple delight of a child at bedtime, to the probing of the adult mind and heart into the deepest mysteries of life.

This collection brings together some of the wisdom stories from around the world. They spring from many different cultures, yet they speak a universal language, and in many cases they reappear in slightly different guises in the oral traditions of many nations. The stories in this book are arranged in sections that focus on different aspects of the human search for truth and meaning: our sense of our own destiny; the treasure that is to be found in the minutiae of everyday living; the triumph of good over evil; the lasting values that determine how we live; warnings of the consequences of wrongdoing; illustrations of what it means to live true to the best within us; examples of patience and determination in the face of hardship; tales of sacrifice; and stories of what it means to be in right relationship with each other and with the whole of creation.

Stories, above all else, are there to be *enjoyed*. It is my hope that you will enjoy the stories in this collection, and that they will also lead you closer to who you truly are and what you most desire. May they serve as companions on your own journey of exploration into the meaning of human life, whether you make this journey mainly on your own or with like-minded companions, whether you are engaged simply in your personal journeying or guiding others – young or old – in the discovery of their own wisdom.

For this, ultimately, is the purpose of all stories – to help us to discover our own story, and to live true to its wisdom.

Margaret Silf

Destiny

1

A Beautiful Friendship

There was once a beautiful woman who used to walk through the streets of the town, and everywhere she went she was noticed. Everyone in town wanted to talk to her, listen to her, ask her questions, and spend time with her. In the same town, there was a poor girl, dressed in rags. She too was very beautiful, but no one ever noticed her or wanted to have anything to do with her. She was lonely and sad. She would gaze at the beautiful, finely dressed woman and see how much attention everyone paid to her. And she wished so much that people would pay attention to *her*. She had so much in her heart that she wanted to share, but no one would listen.

So one day, the poor little girl in rags plucked up courage to speak to the beautiful lady in the fine clothes. 'Please,' she said timidly, 'excuse me, but may I ask you a favour?' The fine lady, who was a very kind person, turned around at once and smiled at the poor girl.

'Of course,' she replied. 'What can I do for you?'

'Well,' ventured the poor girl, 'it's like this: you are very beautiful and finely dressed, and everyone takes notice of you, but I am poor and have no fine clothes, and no one ever even notices me. It would make me so happy if, just for one day, I might hide myself inside your beautiful cloak and walk around with you through the town. Then, whenever people stopped to notice you, they would also be paying attention to me, and I think I have something important to tell them that they would value, if only they knew.'

The fine, elegant lady readily agreed to the poor girl's request, so the very next morning, she wrapped her fine cape around the poor girl, and they walked together through the town. Everywhere, as usual, people stopped to admire the fine lady, and when they did so, they also paid attention to the poor girl wrapped in the fine lady's clothing. As they walked, the fine lady talked with the poor girl. She asked all about her, and was very interested in everything she had to say. She discovered just how wise the poor, ragged girl actually was, and they quickly became the best of friends – so much so that, after that day, they never wanted to be parted. To this day, they still walk through the world together.

And the name of the poor little girl in rags? She is called Truth. And her great friend in the beautiful clothes, whom everyone admires? Her name is Story.

Retelling of a traditional story

Geronimo Grub

'I wonder where the old frog goes,' Geronimo the grub pondered one day. 'He swims to the top of the pond and disappears from sight till – plop! There he is again.'

'Why don't you ask him yourself?' suggested a minnow mischievously. For the frog didn't have much patience with young grubs. But Geronimo summoned up his courage.

'Respected frog, sir,' he began politely, 'if you please, sir, there is something I would like to ask you.'

'I don't please,' replied the frog. 'But ask away, ask away, if you must.'

'Well, sir,' Geronimo said very shyly, 'can you tell me what there is beyond this world?'

'Well, I'll tell you,' replied the frog scornfully. 'There is dry land. Dry land with green grass and meadows filled with golden buttercups and sweet white daisies; and there are blue skies and dreamy white clouds and brilliant sunshine.'

'Wow!' exclaimed Geronimo. He could not imagine a world beyond the dark pond waters. 'Dry land?' he repeated wonderingly. 'Can you swim in it?'

'Of course not!' chuckled the frog. 'Dry land is not water – that is just what it is not!' And he blew some bubbles to show his amusement.

'Well, what is it then?' Geronimo persisted.

'You really are the most inquisitive creature I have ever come across. Since you're so eager to find out what lies above, I'll give you a ride upon my back and you can see for yourself,' the frog offered, exasperated by all the questions.

Geronimo was delighted. He climbed onto the frog's back and up they went!

But the moment they reached the surface – crash! He reeled back into the pond, gasping for breath. He clung to the stem of a water plant, trembling with shock and disappointment, until the frog joined him.

'There is nothing beyond this pond but death,' he wept. 'Why did you tell me all those stories about beautiful colours and bright light?'

'I told you those "stories", as you call them,' the frog said sternly, 'because they are true. You know only this little pond, so you will not believe there is anything beyond it.' And he swam away.

Geronimo did not see the frog for many days. But as the days grew warmer, Geronimo began to feel strange. His eyes became large and brilliant and some extraordinary force seemed to be urging him upwards, upwards! He began struggling slowly up a bulrush stem towards the surface. His brothers gathered round anxiously, begging him not to go. 'Don't leave us!' they cried.

'I must go,' he gasped.

'Then promise you will come back and tell us what lies beyond. Don't forget us,' they implored.

'Never!' Geronimo answered firmly. 'I will never forget you. I will return and tell you what I have seen.' And then he was gone.

His brothers waited for days, but he never came back. At last they gave up hope of ever seeing him again. 'He has forgotten us,' they said bitterly.

Geronimo had not forgotten his brothers, but he could not return to them. He had become a dazzling dragonfly, and risen with glittering wings into the sunshine. He could fly over the green meadow with its golden buttercups and sweet white daisies. He could soar into the blue skies.

No, Geronimo would not forget his brothers. One day, they too would leave the pond. And one day they would fly free together.

Abridged from a retelling by Pat Wynnejones

The Pearl

Many ages ago, almost before time began, there lived an oyster. For all her life, the oyster had been in the sandy ocean bed, moving aimlessly in the mud at the depths of the ocean.

Then one night, there was a full moon, and the brilliant moonlight penetrated even those darkest regions of the deep ocean. Somewhere in her depths, the oyster became aware of the brilliant light filtering down through the water, touching the very core of her being, even through her hard outer shell. In some way that she could not understand, she was profoundly attracted by the mysterious glow, and drawn, as if by a magnet, to the surface of the water and the source of the light.

Steadily, she rose through the waters. As she broke the surface, she was overcome by the glory of the light, now sensed with a directness that had been impossible underwater. It was a glory and a power that invited her, irresistibly, to open herself to its overwhelming presence. Her shell loosened under its spell, just enough to trap a fragment of the moonlight within her innermost self for all eternity.

She was a mortal creature, and her vision could only last for a fleeting moment. The waves drew her down again to the ocean floor. But the pearl was formed within her, conceived in the heavenly encounter, and it began to grow, slowly, imperceptibly, through all her years.

The oyster grew old, never forgetting the treasure she held inside her heart, at the core of her being. But then a grey day dawned, and the ocean was wild and turbulent. The shadow of a fishing boat cast its gloom across the ocean bed. Before she could take in what was happening to her, the oyster was caught up in the net of death, and swept out of the water. Her heart sank. The pearl inside her trembled for fear. She shivered at the bottom of the fishing boat, dreading what was going to happen to her.

Night fell. The storm abated, and the full moon once more shed its light over the quietened ocean, like a great Mother-of-Pearl in the inky skies. Even as the old oyster gazed up one last time, from the depths of the boat, at the skies above the earth, she felt herself gathered up in the gentle hands of the Pearl-Maker.

She held her breath as the Pearl-Maker took her between his fingers, prised open her shell, encrusted now with the experience of all her years, and looked with love upon the pearl that he had made. 'I have been waiting for you, little pearl,' he murmured. 'Without you, my eternal necklace could not be completed.' And he carried her, with infinite tenderness, to a vast circle of pearls that stretched far beyond the horizon, each one uniquely cherished by its maker. He joined her to the circle of light, and he placed the shimmering necklace around the earth.

To this day, the earth is surrounded by the halo of pearls in a ring of eternal light.

Retelling of a traditional story

4

The Artist

One bright, sunny day, two pieces of paper were sunbathing in the midday warmth, enjoying the pleasures of the summertime. One piece of paper was called Snow-White. She was pure white, and so very proud of her pristine purity. 'Look at me,' she said to her companion. 'Did you ever see such a beautifully white piece of paper?' Her companion was called Pure-as-the-Dawn. She too was amazingly white and wonderfully free from the slightest stain. The two pieces of paper outshone each other in the midday sunlight.

In the distance, a figure appeared upon the horizon. He caught their attention. As they watched, he approached, ever closer.

'Who can that be?' asked Snow-White.

'What is he carrying in his arms?' wondered Pure-as-the-Dawn.

The figure came closer and closer, until he was only a few yards away from the two paper-friends.

In his arms, he carried a palette and paintbrushes. In his eyes, there was a curious, dream-like light. A love-light, but gentle. And in his heart, he carried a dream.

'What do you think he wants?' Snow-White asked Pure-as-the-Dawn. 'You don't think he is going to paint on us, do you?'

Pure-as-the-Dawn flinched, as the words sank in. 'I think that is exactly what he wants to do,' she murmured.

'There's no way that I will allow him to paint on me,' railed Snow-White. 'No painter is going to spoil my purity.'

'But what if he is a master-painter?' Pure-as-the-Dawn reflected. 'He might create a masterpiece on our pure white emptiness. He might make *us* into masterpieces.'

'But then again,' said Snow-White, 'he might make a complete mess of us. No. I'm not taking any risks like that. I'm going to stay pure until the day I die.'

And so it came to be that the artist approached both pieces of paper and asked their permission to paint his dream upon their pure whiteness.

Snow-White said, 'No way!' And she remained pure white, and empty, until the day that the wind and the weather finally turned her back into pulp.

Pure-as-the-Dawn said, 'Do as you will with me. I will trust you. I will entrust myself to the work of your hands.' And the artist turned her into a masterpiece – a unique and beautiful representation of the dream that he was carrying in his heart, so that in all the years to come many, many people would look at the artist's picture, and in its depths and beauty, they would rediscover their own lost dreams.

Retelling of a traditional story

5

The Salt Doll

A doll of salt, after a long pilgrimage on dry land, came to the sea and discovered something she had never seen and could not possibly understand. She stood on firm ground, a solid little doll of salt, and saw there was another ground that was mobile, insecure, noisy, strange and unknown.

She asked the sea, 'But what are you?'

It replied, 'I am the sea.'

And the doll said, 'I cannot understand, but I want to. How can I?'

The sea answered, 'Touch me.'

So the doll shyly put a foot forwards and touched the water, and she gained the impression that the sea was beginning to be knowable. She withdrew her leg, looked down and saw that her toe had gone. She was afraid and said, 'Oh, but where is my toe? What have you done to me?'

And the sea said, 'You have given something in order to understand.'

Gradually, the water took away small bits of the doll's salt, and the doll went further and further into the sea. At every moment, she had a sense of understanding more and more, and yet of not being able to say what the sea was. As she went deeper and deeper, she dissolved more and more, repeating, 'But what is the sea?'

At last, a wave dissolved the rest of her and the doll said, 'It is I.'

She had discovered what the sea was, but not yet what the water was. The doll knew what the sea was when she became – minute as she was – the vastness of the sea.

Retelling of a story by Anthony de Mello

6

Becoming Real

The Skin Horse had lived longer in the nursery than any of the others. He was so old that his brown coat was bald in patches and showed the seams underneath, and most of the hairs in his tail had been pulled out to string bead necklaces. He was wise, for he had seen a long succession of mechanical toys arrive to boast and swagger, and by and by break their mainsprings and pass away, and he knew they were only toys, and would never turn into anything else. For nursery magic is very strange and wonderful, and only those playthings that are old and wise and experienced like the Skin Horse understand all about it.

'What is REAL?' asked the Rabbit one day, when they were lying side by side near the nursery fender, before Nana came to tidy the room. 'Does it mean having things that buzz inside you and a stick-out handle?'

'Real isn't how you are made,' said the Skin Horse. 'It's a thing that happens to you. When a child loves you for a long time, not just to play with, but REALLY loves you, then you become Real.'

'Does it hurt?' asked the Rabbit.

'Sometimes,' said the Skin Horse, for he was always truthful. 'When you are Real you don't mind being hurt.'

'Does it happen all at once, like being wound up,' the Rabbit asked, 'or bit by bit?'

'It doesn't happen all at once,' said the Skin Horse. 'You become. It takes a long time. That's why it doesn't often happen to people who break easily, or have sharp edges, or have to be carefully kept. Generally, by the time you are Real, most of your hair has been loved off, and your eyes drop out and you get loose in the joints and very shabby. But these things don't matter at all, because once you are Real you can't be ugly, except to people who don't understand.'

'I suppose *you* are Real?' said the Rabbit. And then he wished he had not said it, for he thought the Skin Horse might be sensitive. But the Skin Horse only smiled.

'The Boy's Uncle made me Real,' he said. 'That was a great many years ago; but once you are Real you can't become unreal again. It lasts for always.'

Margery Williams

7

What is Life?

One lovely summer's day, around noon, there was a deep stillness over all the forest. The birds had tucked their heads under their wings, and everything was at rest.

Then a bullfinch popped his head up and asked, 'What is life?' Everyone was struck by this profound question.

A rose was just emerging from her bud, and was opening up one shy petal after another, rejoicing in the newly discovered sunlight. 'Life is a Becoming,' she said.

The butterfly was less philosophical. He flew blithely from one flower to another, snacking everywhere on the delicious nectar. 'Life is pure pleasure and sunshine,' he announced.

Down on the ground, an ant was labouring under the weight of a piece of straw ten times his size. He said, 'Life is nothing but toil and sweat and strain.'

There might have been quite an argument about the meaning of life, had not a fine rain begun to fall, and the rain spoke: 'Life consists of tears, nothing but tears.'

High above the forest, an eagle swooped, making majestic curves in the sky. 'Life', spoke the eagle, 'is a constant striving upwards.'

Night fell and soon a man came staggering home from a party. 'Life', he complained, 'is a constant search for happiness, and a string of disappointments.'

After the long, dark night, at last dawn came, rising pink on the eastern skyline. 'Just as I, the dawn, am the start of the new day, so life is the beginning of eternity.'

Retelling of a Swedish legend

8

The Stream

High in the far-off mountains, a little stream sprang from its hidden source. It flowed down the mountainside, through all kinds of different terrain, sometimes leaping and bubbling, sometimes drifting lazily or going underground, but it was never stopped by any obstacle that may have got in its way.

One day, it reached the edge of a vast desert. 'Just one more obstacle to overcome,' it thought to itself. 'Nothing has ever stopped me flowing, and I shall surely overcome this obstacle too.' And so the stream flung itself at the desert. But each time it did so, its waters simply disappeared, trickling away into nothingness, swallowed up by the dry, hot sand.

But the stream was not to be deterred. If its destiny was to cross this desert, then it would surely find a way. 'If the wind can cross the desert, so can the stream,' it thought to itself, and the desert sands seemed to echo back these words: 'The winds cross the desert and so can the stream.'

And so began a conversation between the stream and the desert sand. 'I know I must cross this desert,' the stream told the sand, 'but every time I try, the sand swallows me up. No matter how hard I fling myself at the desert, I don't get any further.'

The desert replied, 'You won't be able to cross the desert using the old methods that worked for you further up the mountain. It is no use hurling yourself at the desert like that. You will never cross the sand like this. You will simply disappear, or turn into marshland. No, you must trust the wind to carry you across the desert. You must let yourself be carried.'

'How can the wind carry me across the desert?' the stream asked in disbelief.

'You must let yourself be absorbed into the wind, and then the wind will carry you,' the desert replied. But the stream didn't like this idea. After all, it was a stream, with a nature and identity of its own. It didn't at all want to lose itself by being absorbed into the wind. The desert sensed the stream's fears, and tried to offer reassurance.

'That's what the wind does,' it told the stream. 'Trust me, and trust the wind. If you let yourself be absorbed by the wind, it will carry you across the desert and let you fall again on the other side, to be a stream again.'

The stream wasn't convinced. 'But I won't be the same stream that I am now. I won't be this particular stream.'

The desert understood the dilemma, but the desert also understood the mystery: 'You certainly won't be the same stream you are now if you fling yourself into the sand and turn into a marsh. But let the wind carry you across the desert, and the real heart of you, the essence of everything you truly are, will be born again on the other side, to flow a new course, to be a river that you can't even imagine from where you are standing now.'

The stream thought for a while, and something deep in its heart had a memory of a wind that could be trusted, and a horizon that was always out of reach, but was always a new beginning. So the stream took a deep breath, and surrendered to the power of the wind.

The wind raised up the vapour of the little stream and carried it in strong and loving arms far beyond the horizon, high above the hot desert sand, and let it fall again softly at the top of a new mountain, far away. And the stream began to understand who it really was, and what it meant to be a stream.

Retelling of a traditional story

The Stone Cutter

Once upon a time there was a stone cutter. Each day, he went up to the mountains to cut stones. And while he worked he sang, for though he was a poor man, he desired no more than he had, so he had not a care in the world.

One day, he was called to work on the mansion of a nobleman. When he saw the magnificence of the mansion, he experienced the pain of desire for the first time in his life, and he said with a sigh, 'If only I were rich! Then I would not have to earn my living in sweat and toil as I do now.'

Imagine his astonishment when he heard a voice say, 'Your wish has been granted. Henceforth, anything you desire will be given to you.' He did not know what to make of the words till he returned to his hut that evening and found in its place a mansion as magnificent as the one he had been working on. So the stone cutter gave up cutting stones and began to enjoy the life of the rich.

One day, when the afternoon was hot and humid, he happened to look out of his window and saw the king go by with a large retinue of noblemen and slaves. He thought, 'How I wish I were a king myself, sitting in the cool of the royal carriage!' His wish was promptly carried out and he found himself reclining in the comfort of the royal carriage. But the carriage turned out to be warmer than he had assumed it to be. He looked out of the carriage window and began to marvel at the power of the sun, whose heat could penetrate even the thick walls of the carriage. 'I wish I were the sun,' he said to himself. Once again his wish was granted and he found himself sending out waves of heat into the universe.

All went well for a while. Then on a rainy day, he attempted to pierce through a thick bank of clouds and could not. So he got himself changed into a cloud and glorified in his power to keep the sun away – till he turned into rain and found, to his annoyance, a mighty rock that blocked his path, so he was obliged to flow around it.

'What?' he cried. 'A mere rock more powerful than I? Well, then, I wish to be a rock.' So there he was standing tall upon a mountainside. He barely had time to rejoice in his fine figure, however, when he heard strange chipping noises proceeding from his feet. He looked down, and to his dismay, found a tiny human being sitting there engaged in cutting chunks of stone from his feet.

'What?' he shouted. 'A puny creature like that more powerful than an imposing rock like me? I want to be a man!' So he found he was once again a stone cutter, going up into the mountain to cut stone, earning his living in sweat and toil – but with a song in his heart, because he was content to be what he was and to live by what he had.

Anthony de Mello

The Land of the Mighty Mountain

There was once a country famed far and wide for its holy mountain. People from all over the world had heard about the holy mountain, but the strange thing was, the people who actually lived in that country had a habit of walking around with their eyes always focused on the ground. They never lifted their heads. And if you asked them what they were doing, they would tell you: 'We are searching for the holy mountain, of course. Why don't you join us in the search? This is where you must look.'

And so they lived their lives, restless, moving round in circles, walking up and down the many lanes and alleyways of their country, poring over their maps and arguing with each other about where, exactly, the holy mountain was to be found.

Meanwhile, the holy mountain soared to the skies, waiting patiently for the people to discover its beauty and its power, and saddened to watch them picking their way through the world and never stopping to look up.

In one part of the country, there was a large lake, with water as smooth as glass. The mountain was reflected in this lake, and many of the people of that country would gather around the lake, point to the reflection and claim that they had discovered the mountain. Some of them jumped into the lake and were drowned. Others thought that the mountain had an evil influence, and turned away from the lake. Others decided that, after all, there was no such thing as a holy mountain.

Then one day, amid all the hustle and bustle of the people's desperate search for the mountain, one of them fell over, and was almost trampled to death by the milling feet all around him. He lay there, flat on his back, thinking that his end must surely be close, when to his amazement, he looked up and saw the holy mountain towering serenely above him. He tried to tell everyone what he had seen, but no one believed him, so he set off alone to seek out the path that would lead him to the mountain.

It was a hard journey, for the path was sometimes steep and perilous, and he kept losing sight of his goal. Many times he fell in his journeying, and every time he fell, he would see, once more, the mountain he was searching for, and be encouraged to keep on walking. And as he walked, he noticed that the only other people on the path to the mountain were disabled or sick, or were carrying some great load that had made them topple over in their need. He realized that only those who had fallen were ever able to see the mountain, and only those who knew the full meaning of the word 'down' could ever look up.

Source unknown

The Forever Tree

Once, a long, long time ago, a little tree was growing in the forest. As the little tree grew taller and stronger, she began to notice the wide expanse of sky stretching far above her head. She noticed the white clouds scudding across the sky, as if on some great journey. She watched the birds wheeling overhead.

The skies, the clouds, the birds in flight – they all seemed to speak of a land of forever. The more she grew, the more she noticed these forever things, and the more she longed to live forever herself.

One day, the forester happened to pass close by the little tree. He was a kindly man, and he sensed that the little tree was not entirely happy. 'What's the matter, little tree?' he asked. 'What troubles your soul?'

The little tree hesitated, and then told the forester about the deep desire in the core of her being: 'I would so much like to live forever.'

'Perhaps you shall,' replied the forester. 'Perhaps you shall.'

Some time passed, and once again the forester passed close by the little tree, now grown tall and strong.

'Do you still want to live forever?' he asked the tree.

'Oh, I do, I do,' the tree replied fervently.

'I think I can help, but first you must give me your permission to cut you down.'

The tree was aghast: 'I wanted to live forever. And now you say you are going to kill me?'

'I know,' said the forester. 'It sounds crazy. But if you can trust me, I promise you that your deepest desire will be fulfilled.'

After much hard thought, the tree gave her consent. The forester came with his sharp-bladed axe. The tree was felled. The sap of life streamed away and was lost in the forest floor. The tender wood was sliced into strips. The strips were planed and shaped and smothered in a suffocating layer of varnish. The tree screamed silently in her anguish, but there was no way back. She surrendered herself to the hands of the violin-maker, and all dreams of foreverness vanished in a haze of pain.

For many years, the violin lay idle. Sometimes, she remembered better days, when she was growing in the woods. What a bad bargain it had been, surrendering herself to the forester's axe. How could she have been so naive as to believe that this would enable her to live forever?!

But the day came − the right and perfect moment − when the violin was gently lifted from her case and caressed once more by loving hands. She held her breath in disbelief. She quivered as the bow tenderly crossed her breast. And the quivering turned into a pure sound that reminded her of how the wind had once rustled through her leaves, how the clouds had once scudded by on their way to forever, how the birds had wheeled overhead, shaping circles of eternity in the blue sky.

A pure sound. Pure notes. The music of Forever.

'My wood has turned into music!' the tree gasped deep inside herself. 'The forester spoke the truth.'

And the music resounded, from listening heart to listening heart, down through all the ages until at last, when all the listening hearts had made their own journey home, it rolled through the gates of eternity, where the little tree became a Forever Tree.

Margaret Silf

God in Hiding

A legend tells how, at the beginning of time, God resolved to hide himself within his own creation.

As God was wondering how best to do this, the angels gathered round him.

'I want to hide myself in my creation,' he told them. 'I need to find a place that is not too easily discovered, for it is in their search for me that my creatures will grow in spirit and in understanding.'

'Why don't you hide yourself deep in their earth?' the first angel suggested.

God pondered for a while, then replied, 'No. It will not be long before they learn how to mine the earth and discover all the treasures that it contains. They will discover me too quickly, and they will not have had enough time to do their growing.'

'Why don't you hide yourself on their moon?' a second angel suggested.

God thought about this idea for a while, and then replied, 'No. It will take a little longer, but before too long they will learn how to fly through space. They will arrive on the moon and explore its secrets, and they will discover me too soon, before they have had enough time to do their growing.'

The angels were at a loss to know what hiding places to suggest. There was a long silence.

'I know,' piped up one angel, finally. 'Why don't you hide yourself within their own hearts? They will never think of looking there!'

'That's it!' said God, delighted to have found the perfect hiding place. And so it is that God hides secretly deep within the heart of every one of God's creatures, until that creature has grown enough in spirit and in understanding to risk the great journey into the secret core of its own being. And there, the creature discovers its creator, and is rejoined to God for all eternity.

Retelling of a traditional story

Treasure in Everyday Life

The Good King

There was once a very good king who lived in a beautiful country, where the sun was always shining and the people were always happy. There was a river that ran around his country, and on the other side of it, there was a country that was completely different! It had hardly any sun, a great deal of rain and cold wind, and a wicked, cruel king who made everybody miserable. So the good king built a long bridge over the river, and asked the unhappy people to come over and live with him. The strange thing was that the people didn't want to come. They said they couldn't find the bridge, that it was too much trouble to go across, and that some of them lived too far away from it to find it.

So one day, the king sent three of his servants over to show the people the way, and to tell them about it. Two of these servants had a great talent; the third thought herself very stupid, but she loved her king, and told him she would do her best.

The first one of the servants went into the unhappy country and began to sing to the people. She had a beautiful voice, and wherever she went the people gathered in crowds to hear her. She sang of the king and of the happy country over the bridge, and as she sang the people felt they wanted to go there. But sometimes, when she stopped singing, the people stopped wanting to go. And some only cared for her voice, and not for her message.

The second servant reached even more people than the first, because she wrote her message, and she had a wonderful pen. Far, far away, people read her letters and writings, and they liked them, for she was given the power to touch their hearts. But sometimes, she altered her message a little to please the people more, and the way across the bridge to the beautiful country was not mentioned so often; sometimes, it was nearly hidden altogether, and the people thought they could make their own country as nice as the other one, without troubling to go across the bridge. But she wrote on, and the singer sang on, and both were trying to obey their king.

And the little stupid servant? Ah, the third servant! She couldn't sing, and she couldn't write, and she couldn't reach very many people. But her little heart was full of love for her king, and so she talked about him to everyone who would listen to her. She wasn't clever, but she said a word here and a word there, and she always kept pointing to the bridge. Little children found their way easily when she took them by the hand and led them there. Old men and women leaned on her arm, and hobbled slowly towards it. She would whisper softly to the weeping ones, she would explain slowly to the stupid ones, and everybody listened to her, because they said she was so simple and clear, and didn't confuse them. She only knew one bridge, and she always pointed to it, and talked of the good king.

By and by, the king called his servants home. When they came back, he called together all those to whom the servants had shown the way. The singer was met by a small number of people, who told her that they had found the bridge by her singing. The writer was met also by some who, far away, had read her message, and had been guided to the bridge by it. But the little stupid servant was surrounded by a crowd! Her halting words had brought more over to the beautiful country than the wonderful messages of the clever ones. And the king smiled upon her, and said, 'The singer has done well, and so has the writer, but the little speaker has done the best of all!'

Amy le Feuvre

The Leaky Bucket

There was once a beautiful garden. The gardener was very proud of his garden, and he cared for it with great tenderness. Every day, he would make the journey to his little garden shed at the far end of the garden, and there he would fill up his buckets with clear, sparkling water from the nearby stream. Then he would walk along the little pathway to where the flower beds were, carrying water for the flowers.

To water his flowers, he used two buckets, which he kept in the garden shed. One was a bright, shiny, new bucket, recently bought from the garden centre. One was a very old and rather dilapidated bucket, which had seen long years of service in the garden, but was now well past its best.

The gardener would fill up the two buckets every morning and carry them along, side by side, to the flower beds. The bright, shiny bucket was very proud of itself. It could be relied upon to carry the full consignment of water right up to the flower beds without spilling a single drop. The shabby, old bucket felt very ashamed in comparison. It knew it had holes in it, and every morning it was so sad to see that by the time the gardener reached the flower beds, a good deal of its water had already spilled out along the path, and was wasted.

Sometimes, the two buckets would talk to each other as the gardener carried them along the path to the flower beds.

'See how efficient I am,' the shiny bucket would boast. 'How good that the gardener has me to make sure that the flowers are watered every day. I don't know why he still bothers with you. You're a waste of space.'

And all that the shabby, old bucket could say was, 'I know I'm not much use, but I can only do my best. I'm happy that the gardener still finds a little bit of use for me, at least.'

One day, the gardener heard this kind of conversation going on. When he reached the flower beds, he watered the flowers as usual, using the full bucket of water from the shiny bucket, and the half-bucket of water that was still left in the leaky, old bucket. Then he picked up both buckets, now empty, and said to them, 'Thank you both. You have done your day's work very well. Now I am going to carry you back to the shed, but as we go, I want you to look carefully at the pathway.'

So the two buckets did as the gardener asked them. And they noticed that all along the path on one side – the side where the gardener carried the shiny, new bucket – there was just bare earth. But on the other side – the side where the gardener carried the leaky, old bucket – there was a row of young, fresh, green shoots, which, in another few weeks, would be a joyous row of wild flowers, leading all the way to the garden.

Retelling of a traditional story

Natural Treasure

Paddy grew the finest gooseberries, blackcurrants and redcurrants in the whole country. He had three fields of fruit bushes, and every day he walked round the bushes with a hoe, taking out any weeds which were growing, so the bushes had all the goodness of the soil to themselves. By the middle of each summer they were heavy with large, juicy fruit.

But sadly, Paddy was not as good at raising children as he was at raising fruit. His two sons were known as the laziest young men in the country. They spent all day drinking, eating and chatting with friends; they never lifted a finger to help their father. As the years passed, Paddy became increasingly anxious about his sons' laziness.

'When I am dead and gone,' he would say to his neighbours, 'all my fruit bushes will become overgrown with weeds, and my sons will starve.'

Living a short distance from the village in a small cave was a hermit, renowned for his wily wisdom. Finally Paddy decided to visit this hermit, to ask advice. After he heard Paddy's story, the hermit sat for a few moments in silence, stroking his long, white beard. At last the hermit rose up, patted Paddy on the shoulder, and assured him that he would teach the two lazy sons to work. Then the hermit left his hut, and went to see the young men.

'I have something very important to tell you,' he said to them. 'I happen to know that in those fields of fruit bushes there is great treasure. It will be enough to feed and clothe you for the rest of your lives.'

It was now September. From then until Christmas, the two sons went out into the fields each day searching for treasure. They dug round every fruit bush, turning over the earth, in the hope of finding a casket full of gold. But by Christmas Eve they had found nothing. So they went to the hermit, and accused him of deceiving them.

'I haven't deceived you,' the hermit replied with a grin. 'You must keep searching. I promise that by next September you will have found the treasure.'

The sons refused to believe him.

'Very well, then,' the hermit continued; 'I will make a bargain with you. If by September you have not found enough treasure to buy food and clothing for you for the rest of your lives, I will share whatever I receive with you. But if you do find treasure, you must share it with the poor in this village.'

The brothers agreed. So they continued to dig the fields, turning over the earth between the fruit bushes. Paddy watched with great satisfaction, pleased that while his sons searched for treasure, no weeds would grow. Thus, by the middle of summer, the bushes were again heavy with large and juicy fruit. The hermit came to the fields to see the two sons.

'Ah,' he exclaimed, looking at the fruit bushes, 'I see you have found your treasure.'

At first, the two sons could not think what he meant. Then it dawned on them. Over the next few weeks, the hermit helped them to pick the treasure. Half they sold in the market, and the other half they gave to the poor.

And from then on, the two brothers continued to work hard in the fields. Each year, they again sold half the crop and gave away the rest. And as the hermit had prophesied, the money they got was quite sufficient to feed and clothe them for the rest of their lives.

Robert van de Weyer

Men at Work

During the Middle Ages, a traveller once came upon a place in France where a great deal of building work was going on. He began talking with the stone cutters and asking them about their work.

He approached the first worker and asked, 'What are you doing?'

The man, very disgruntled, and obviously unhappy in his hard toil, replied, 'I'm cutting these huge boulders with the simplest of tools and putting them together in the way I've been told to do. I'm sweating in this heat and my back is hurting. What's more, I'm totally bored, and I wish I didn't have to do this hard and meaningless job.'

The traveller moved on quickly to interview a second worker. He asked the same question: 'What are you doing?'

The worker replied, 'Well, I have a wife and children at home, so I come here every morning and I work these boulders into regular shapes, as I'm told to do. It gets repetitive sometimes, but it helps to feed my family, and that's all I want.'

Somewhat encouraged, the traveller went on to a third worker. 'And what are *you* doing?' he asked.

The third worker responded with shining eyes, as he pointed up to the heavens, 'I'm building a cathedral!'

Source unknown

17

The Magic Vase

There was once a poor family who lived in a drab little house in the neglected part of the city. They tried to be a happy family, but times were hard, and jobs were not easy to come by. As time went on, they began to feel more and more depressed. You could see their depression etching itself even on the house they lived in. They no longer bothered to clean the windows. They didn't tend the little patch of garden in front of the house. The paint peeled off the door and cracks appeared in the brickwork.

One day, the eldest son of the family was roaming idly through the town and he came upon a market place. The stallholders had set up their wares, and there was a bustle of activity. In spite of his feelings of near despair, the boy found himself being caught up in the excitement of the morning market.

He stopped to watch the people buying fruit and vegetables, freshly baked bread and tempting cakes. He noticed the queue at the fish stall, and took a deep breath of pleasure as he passed the stall of fresh summer flowers.

But the stall that attracted him most was a little second-hand stall, tucked away among the awnings of the regular marketeers. He had never noticed this stall before. He stopped to investigate. And there, hidden away in the dark recesses, he noticed a beautiful vase.

Rapidly, he fingered the coins in his pocket. He had just enough to meet the modest cost of the vase, but there would be nothing left over. 'Ah well,' he thought to himself. 'Why not? Even if we have a few lean days, I am going to buy this vase. Mum will love it. Everyone will love it.' And he handed over the contents of his pocket to the man behind the counter.

As he wrapped the vase in brown paper, the stallholder said to the boy, 'Enjoy it, won't you? And treat it well, because it is a magic vase.' With these mysterious words ringing in his ears, the lad went off home, proudly carrying his purchase.

Everyone at home was delighted with the vase, and no one reproached him for spending his last few coins on it. Quite the opposite, in fact.

When Dad saw the vase, he realized how shabby the room was, and he went to the cellar, got out the paintbrushes, and gave the room a makeover. And when the second son saw how nice the room looked, with its fresh coat of paint, he fetched a bucket of water and washed the windows, for the first time in years. When the third son looked out of the bright new windows, he realized what a state the garden was in, and went outside to dig it over. When the fourth son saw the newly dug garden, he planted seeds in the flower bed and watered them lovingly, all through the spring. When summer came and the young daughter of the family went out to play in the garden, she noticed the flowers that had grown from the seeds, and she gathered a bunch of them to give to her mother.

'Here are some pretty flowers, Mummy,' she said, 'because we love you.' Mum was overjoyed. With tears rising in her eyes, and a lump in her throat, she put the flowers in the magic vase.

Retelling of a traditional story

The Making of a Saint

Johnny was out shopping with his mother one morning in the high street. Feeling a bit bored, he happened to look up at the windows of the nearby cathedral. He wasn't very impressed. From the outside, they looked drab and dull and a bit grimy. He said as much to his mother when she came out of the supermarket.

'Just let's go inside,' she said to him. So they went into the cathedral, and his mother took him to where the big stained-glass windows were.

At first, Johnny was entranced by the magical coloured patterns on the stone floor of the ancient church. They seemed to dance in front of him as the morning light streamed through the mighty windows.

'Look at that,' he pointed to the dancing image on the stone floor. 'What is it, Mum?'

'Well,' his mother replied, 'actually, that's a saint. See the window up there, which looked so dull from the outside? There's a saint up there in the stained glass, and the light is shining through her and making her picture dance for us here on the stone floor.'

Johnny stored up this information in his heart, and the two of them went home for dinner.

A few days later, Johnny's class was having a religious instruction lesson. The teacher was talking about saints. 'What do you think makes a saint?' he asked the class.

Johnny's hand shot up. 'A saint is someone the sun shines through,' he explained, 'and when that happens, the stones come to life.'

Source unknown

Hidden Treasure

Once upon a time, there lived the old Rabbi Eisik in a wretched little tenement flat in the city of Krakow in Poland. Eisik lived in extreme poverty with his wife and children. Through all the hard times, Eisik had kept his faith and looked after his family as best he could.

And so it was that he believed, when he had a dream one night, that the dream contained a message from God. In the dream, he had a vision of a chest of gold, hidden beneath a particular bridge in the grounds of the royal palace in Prague.

At first, he hesitated to believe in what he had dreamed. But when the dream recurred a second time, and then a third time, he decided to make the journey to Prague.

But when he found the bridge of his dreams, he saw that it was guarded day and night by sentries, and he didn't dare to start digging. Nevertheless, he came to the bridge every morning, and walked around it all day until evening.

Eventually, the chief guard, noticing the rabbi's odd behaviour, asked him, in a very friendly way, whether he was searching for something there, or perhaps waiting for someone.

Something prompted Rabbi Eisik to tell the friendly guard about the dream that had brought him all the way to Prague from Krakow. The guard laughed. 'Oh dear,' he said. 'You poor old fellow with your worn-out shoes – you have tramped all this way for the sake of a dream! Well, more fool you for trusting a dream. I can tell you that if dreams were to be trusted, then I'd be on the road as well, because I once had a dream that told me to walk to Krakow, and to search out a hovel in the poorest district, belonging to someone called Rabbi Eisik. There I was supposed to search behind the stove, where

I would find hidden treasure. Just imagine how I was supposed to find that treasure in a strange town, where there must be hundreds of Rabbi Eisiks!' And he laughed again.

Rabbi Eisik bowed graciously, and turned back home, to find the treasure hidden closer to him than he could ever have imagined.

Retelling of a traditional East European story

20

The Secret Recipe

When God created mothers, it was well into overtime on the sixth day. An angel dropped by and commented, 'Lord, you are taking your time over this creature!'

God replied, 'You should see the special requirements in the specification! She has to be easy to maintain, but not made of plastic or have any artificial components. She has one hundred and sixty movable parts, and nerves of steel, with a lap big enough for ten children to sit on it at once, but she herself has to be able to fit into a child's chair. She has to have a back that can carry everything that is loaded onto it. She has to be able to mend everything, from a grazed knee to a broken heart. And she's supposed to have six pairs of hands.'

The angel shook her head. 'Six pairs of hands? No way!'

'The hands are easy,' God said. 'But I'm still working on the three pairs of eyes that she needs.'

'Is this the standard model?' the angel asked.

God nodded: 'Oh yes. One pair to look through closed doors, while she asks, "What are you doing?" even though she already knows the answer. A second pair at the back of her head, to see what she's not meant to see, but needs to know about. And, of course, the pair at the front that can look at her child, let him know that he is behaving badly and had better change his ways, while at the same time letting him see how much she loves and understands him.'

'I think you should go to bed now, Lord, and get some sleep,' said the angel.

'I can't do that,' said God. 'I'm almost there. I have nearly created a being who heals herself when she's ill, who can delight thirty children with one little birthday cake, who can persuade a three-year-old not to eat clay, a six-year-old to wash his hands before meals and a nine-year-old to use his feet to walk and not to kick.'

The angel walked slowly around the prototype Mum. 'It's too soft,' she said.

'But tough,' God retorted. 'You wouldn't believe the wear and tear this Mum will tolerate.'

'Can she think?' asked the angel.

'Not only think, but reach wise judgments and essential compromises,' said God. 'And she can do more than that. She can forget!'

Finally, the angel ran her finger across the model's cheek.

'There's a leak,' she said. 'I warned you that you were trying to get too much into her.'

'That's not a leak,' said God. 'That's a tear.'

'What's that for?' asked the angel.

'It flows whenever she feels joy or grief, disappointment or pride, pain or loneliness, or the depths of love.'

'You're a genius,' said the angel.

God looked again at his work of art, with pleasure and pride.

'The tear', he said, 'is her overflow valve.'

Source unknown

The Optimist and the Pessimist

Once upon a time, there were two little boys. One was an optimist. The other was a pessimist.

The two boys each had their own playroom. The little pessimist had a room full of toys. Every Christmas and every birthday, his family and friends brought new toys for him to play with, but each time he would sit in the middle of the room and start to cry, because he had no drum. He wanted a drum so much that he was forever disappointed. The toys lay scattered around him, untouched and unappreciated.

The little optimist wasn't so lucky. All that he had in his playroom was a pile of manure from the farmyard and a fork.

It happened that the boys' parents came past one day and looked into the playrooms where their sons were playing. As usual, the little pessimist was howling because he couldn't find a drum among the vast pile of toys that surrounded him.

But when they looked into the room where the little optimist was playing, they found a happy child, eagerly digging through the pile of manure with his fork. His eyes were alive with excitement, and he was singing as he played. 'With all this manure around,' they heard him say, 'there's got to be a pony in here somewhere!'

Source unknown

The Zither

There was once a good and sincere man who was searching for the way to happiness, searching for the way to truth. One day, he went to seek out a wise old man who, so he had been assured, would be able to show him the way he was searching for.

The wise old man received him warmly, as he sat at the door of his tent. After serving the seeker a glass of mint tea, the wise old man readily revealed the secret of the route to happiness and truth.

'It's a long way from here, to be sure,' he said. 'But you can't miss it. You will come to a village that I will describe to you, and right at the heart of that village, you will find three little shops. There, the secret of happiness and of truth will be revealed to you.'

It was indeed a very long way. The seeker passed along many valleys and across many rivers. Eventually, he arrived at the village, where his heart told him, 'This is the place. Yes, this is the place you are seeking.'

And sure enough, there in the heart of the village were three little shops. But when he went inside them the seeker was deeply disappointed. In the first shop, all he found were some reels of wire. In the second, there was nothing more exciting than a few pieces of wood. And in the third, there was just some roughly shaped metal.

Weary and discouraged, he left the village again, and found a resting place for the night in a little clearing not too far away. Night fell. The full moon filled the clearing with a gentle glow. And just as he was on the point of falling asleep, the searcher heard a sublime melody coming from the direction of the village. What magical instrument could be giving rise to such perfect harmony?

Quickly, he rose to his feet and walked towards where he thought the musician must be. And there, to his amazement, he discovered that the celestial music was coming from a man playing a zither. And the zither, he could plainly see, had been made from the wire, the wood and the metal pieces he had so despised earlier in the day, when he had seen them for sale in the three little shops in the village.

At that moment, he understood that happiness is the union of everything that has already been given to us.

Retelling of a traditional story

The Golden Ball

There was once a little boy who lived in a cottage with his parents. He often used to play out on the hills, and when it began to grow dark, he would go home.

One evening, as he was just returning home, the little boy lingered for a while at the door. Far away, across the valley, he saw a beautiful golden ball. He was spellbound. What could it be, and who might own something so beautiful? That day, he made up his mind that he must make the journey to the other side of the valley, to find his treasure.

And so it happened that one morning he packed his little rucksack with some sandwiches and an apple, and set off to make the journey to the other side of the valley. It took him all day. He had never been so far before, and it took him a lot longer than he had thought it would. By the time he arrived, it was late afternoon, and he was feeling very tired, and hungry. Eventually, very close to the place where he had hoped to find the golden ball, he came upon a little cottage, with smoke curling up out of the chimney, and roses climbing around the doorway. But there was no sign of the golden ball. Shyly, he knocked at the door.

The family from the other side of the valley were very happy to see him – though a little bit surprised, if the truth were told. 'You must be hungry!' the mother exclaimed. 'You are very welcome to eat with us.'

'Where do you come from?' the children asked excitedly, and the little boy pointed across the valley, to his own little home on the hill, now cloaked in darkness.

'It's far too late for you to make the long journey home again tonight,' said the father.

'We'll make you up a bed in the corner,' said the mother.

And so the little boy from across the valley spent the night with his new friends, and as the evening shadows grew longer, they all sat around the kitchen fire, while he told them about the golden ball that he had seen so often from his own home, and asked them where he might find it.

'We've never seen a golden ball like that over here,' they told him, puzzled. 'But tomorrow morning, when the sun is rising, we'll show you *our* treasure.'

The little boy could hardly wait until the morning. When dawn arrived, the children took him to their doorway, and pointed out their treasure. 'Look over there,' they said, pointing straight at his own home on the opposite hillside. 'Can you see our golden ball?' And sure enough, there was a little golden ball to be seen, shining out from his very own cottage, where the rising sun was reflected back from his own bedroom window. 'One day, we will go to the other side of the valley, and find *our* golden ball,' his new friends told him. The little boy smiled.

Source unknown

The Triumph
of Good
Over Evil

The Cave

There was once a dark cave, deep down in the ground, underneath the earth and hidden away from view. Because it was so deep in the earth, the light had never been there. The cave had never seen light. The word 'light' meant nothing to the cave, who couldn't imagine what 'light' might be.

Then one day the sun sent an invitation to the cave, inviting it to come up and visit.

When the cave came up to visit the sun it was amazed and delighted, because the cave had never seen light before, and it was dazzled by the wonder of the experience.

Feeling so grateful to the sun for inviting it to visit, the cave wanted to return the kindness, and so it invited the sun to come down to visit it sometime, because the sun had never seen darkness.

So the day came, and the sun came down and was courteously shown into the cave.

As the sun entered the cave, it looked around with great interest, wondering what 'darkness' would be like. Then it became puzzled, and asked the cave, 'Where is the darkness?'

Source unknown

The Long-Handled Spoons

A rabbi asked God to give him a glimpse of what heaven and hell would be like.

God agreed to this request, and asked the prophet Elijah to be the rabbi's guide on this adventure.

Elijah first led the rabbi into a large room. In the middle of the room was a fire with a big cooking pot bubbling away on it. And in the pot was a delicious stew.

All around the cooking pot sat a crowd of people. They each had a long-handled spoon, which they were dipping into the delicious stew.

But the people looked pale and thin and wretched. There was an icy stillness in the room. The handles of the spoons were so long that no one was able to get the lovely food into their mouth.

When the two visitors were back outside again, the rabbi asked Elijah what strange place this was. 'That was hell,' Elijah explained.

Then Elijah led the rabbi to a second room, which looked exactly like the first. In the middle, a fire was blazing and a cooking pot was bubbling away, full of the same delicious, aromatic stew. People sat around the fire, with the same long-handled spoons in their hands. But they were enjoying lively, animated conversations with each other.

And the difference? Well, the people in the second room were not trying to feed themselves with the long-handled spoons. They were using the spoons to feed each other. 'Ah, heaven,' said the rabbi.

Source unknown

The Old Man's Will

In a small American town, there once lived an old man. Generations of children grew up listening to his stories, and he was always first in line if anyone was in any kind of need. He taught the children to hunt and fish, and everyone loved him. He lived alone in a little log cabin, and his door was always open to all comers.

Now it happened that a valuable seam of copper was discovered, which ran right through the plot of land where the old man had his cabin. Soon, the big businessmen in town approached him. They wanted to buy his land and knock down his cabin, so that they could begin mining the copper.

But the old man didn't understand about money, and their offer had no meaning for him. All he wanted was his own little cabin, right there in the woods, where he had always lived.

The businessmen grew frustrated. After all, a large operation was in jeopardy here, and they stood to make huge profits from the copper mine. When the old man refused to listen to their offers, they began to threaten him. The people who had always been his friends were turning into his enemies. Eventually, they told him in no uncertain terms, 'Unless you are out of this place by sunset, we will come and kill you.' The only person who cared about the old man any more was the town's preacher. He saw what was going on, and made up his mind to do something about it.

Well, sunset came, and the old man was still in his cabin. Meanwhile, however, the town's preacher had slipped off to the cabin, and when the lynch mob arrived to kill the old man, the preacher stepped out of the cabin door, and addressed them quietly.

'The old man realizes he is going to die,' he told them, 'and he has asked me to come out tonight on his behalf and read you his last will and testament.'

The attackers fell silent, and waited impatiently as the preacher unfolded a piece of parchment and began to read:

'I leave my fishing rod to you, Pete, because I remember the first bass you ever caught with it when you were seven.

'I leave my rifle to you, James, because I remember how I taught you to shoot with it.

'I leave my tin whistle to you, Harry, so that you won't forget those tunes we used to play in the summer evenings.

'I leave my leather boots to you, Jake, because you used to play with the bootlaces when we were getting ready to go for those long walks together.'

One by one, the few items that the old man possessed were each bequeathed to the person they would mean most to.

And one by one, the would-be attackers – Pete, James, Harry, Jake and all the others – hung their heads and made their way home in the silence of the night.

Source unknown

The Flawed Ruby

There was once a rich and powerful king who had a large and very unusual ruby that was beyond price. This jewel was the basis of his renown, wealth and power. Each day, he would gaze at it with great pride. One day, to his utter consternation, he saw that the ruby had upon it a scratch. Horror of horrors! What was he to do?

He called each of his palace jewellers to come and examine the scratch, and see what could be done to repair it. They were unanimous that nothing could be done without causing further damage.

The king was devastated, and offered a substantial reward to any jeweller who could be found who could repair the king's ruby. Several jewellers came who fancied their chances, but all confessed that there was, indeed, nothing that could be done.

Some days later, one of the king's servants said that he had heard tell of an old retired jeweller in a remote country district who was said to be very experienced in working with damaged gems. So he was duly sent for; and a few days later he arrived, a bent little old man, rather shabbily dressed. The king's courtiers were very scornful and told the king he was wasting his time. But the king insisted that the old man be shown the damaged gem. He looked at it thoughtfully for some time, and then said to the king, 'I cannot repair your ruby, but if you wish, I can make it more beautiful.' The king was a bit sceptical, but he was desperate to have something done, so he agreed. So the old jeweller set to work, cutting and polishing. Some days later, he returned. Upon the king's precious stone he had carved the most delicate rose, its stem being formed by the scratch.

Francis Dewar

Two Mirrors

Satan always takes great delight in creating confusion. To help him do this better, he once had a special kind of mirror made. This mirror shrank the reflections of all the good and beautiful things in the world, and it enlarged all the bad and ugly things. Satan took great pleasure in going round the earth, holding this mirror in front of people's eyes, until there was not a single land, or a single person, who had not seen this distorted view of the world.

One day, Satan was laughing so much over the trouble this mirror had already caused that it slipped out of his hand and shattered into thousands and millions of tiny fragments. And a great storm blew up and carried these fragments to every corner of the world.

Some of the fragments were as small as grains of sand. They lodged in people's eyes, and from then on, these poor people could only see the bad things in the world. The good things shrank until they were almost invisible. Other fragments were gathered up over the years, and made into glasses, and when people wore these glasses, they could never see anything in its proper perspective again.

God was very sad when he saw how damaged people's vision had become, and how so many of them could only see the bad things around them, and had lost sight of all that was good and beautiful. He had an idea for putting everything right again. 'I know what I will do,' he thought to himself. 'My Son is the image of me, he is my true reflection. I will send him into the world. He will reflect my goodness and my justice, and show the world how I long for it to be.'

So Jesus became a mirror for God's people. He reflected God's goodness out to the world, even to thieves and frauds, and to those whom the world despised. He reflected courage and confidence into the hearts of the sick and despairing. He reflected comfort to those in grief, and trust to those whose hearts were crippled by fear.

Many people recognized God's mirror, and followed Jesus. They loved and trusted him. But others were jealous, and felt their own power threatened by the love of God. In the end, they could tolerate him no longer. They plotted against Jesus and killed him. They shattered God's mirror.

And a great storm blew up. It blew millions of fragments of God's mirror to every corner of the world, and it continues to do so today. These fragments lodge in the eyes of many, many people, and whenever this happens, they are able to see God's world again, just as Jesus saw it. The beauty and goodness of God's creation and God's people are the main thing they see, and then they realize that the bad and the ugly are only transient and can be overcome.

Retelling of a story by Hans Christian Andersen

29

How Much Does a Snowflake Weigh?

It was deep winter and the snow was falling steadily upon the hillside.

A tiny mouse crept out of its hole for a little break in its long winter sleep. Drowsily, the little mouse looked around and twitched its whiskers, and would have gone back to sleep inside its hole, had not a tiny voice echoed from somewhere out there in the white winter world: 'Hello, little mouse. Can't you sleep?'

The mouse looked around and caught sight of a tiny bird sitting, shivering, on a bare branch just overhead. 'Hello, Jenny Wren,' said the mouse, pleased to find some company on this bleak day. 'I just came up for a bit of air before I go back to sleep for the rest of the winter.'

But it was so good to find company that for a while the mouse and the wren sat there together, huddled beneath the lowest branches of a pine tree, watching the snow falling and enjoying a little congenial conversation.

'How much do you think a snowflake weighs?' the mouse asked the wren suddenly.

'A snowflake weighs almost nothing,' the wren replied. 'A snowflake is so insignificant, it carries almost no weight at all. How could you possibly weigh a snowflake?'

'Oh, I disagree,' said the mouse. 'In fact, I can tell you that last winter, around this time, I woke up from my winter dreaming and came out here for a breath of fresh air, and because I had no companions and nothing better to do, I sat here counting the snowflakes as they fell. I watched them settling on these branches, and covering the pine needles with a blanket of whiteness. I got as far as two million, four hundred and ninety-two thousand, three hundred and fifty-nine. And then – when the very next snowflake fell and settled on the branch – the branch dropped right down to the ground and all the snow slid off it. So you see, just that one last snowflake weighed enough to make the branch sink down and all the snow slide off. So a snowflake does weigh something. It does make a difference!'

The wren, who was only a tiny little bird herself and didn't think she had much influence on the great big world around her, pondered for a long time over the mouse's story. 'Perhaps', she thought to herself, 'it really is true that just one little voice can make a difference.'

Source unknown

30

The Apple Seed

Long ago, when times were hard, a man was caught stealing food from the market place.

The king was told of this misdemeanour, and he ordered that the man should be hanged for the theft. Preparations were made to carry out the execution, while the man was held in a dark dungeon.

On the day he was due to be hanged, the guards brought the man to the gallows, and he was asked if there was anything he wanted to say before he was put to death.

'Yes,' said the prisoner. 'I have a message for the king. I have a special gift that was passed on to me by my father, who received it from his father. I can plant an apple seed in the ground and it will grow into a flourishing tree overnight, and bear fruit straight away. I just feel that it would be a pity if this secret gift were to die with me before I had passed it on.'

The king was impressed, and he asked the prisoner to tell him the secret and to plant the apple seed before he died.

'I would gladly do so,' said the prisoner, 'but I must warn you that the seed can only be planted by a person who has never been dishonest – never stolen anything or told a lie, or deceived anyone in any way. So, of course, I cannot plant the seed myself, because I am a convicted thief.'

The king called for his prime minister to plant the seed, but the prime minister looked sheepish, and admitted that he had once kept something that did not belong to him, therefore he could not plant the seed.

So the king called for his chief treasurer, whose face at once flushed deep red as he confessed that there had been times when he had not been completely honest in his dealings with the treasury of the country. 'I think, Your Majesty,' the treasurer said, 'that you will have to plant the seed yourself.'

The king hesitated and became very uneasy, recalling how he had deceived his wife and been unfaithful. He hung his head and admitted that he, too, would be unable to plant the seed.

The thief looked around at all three of them. 'You are the mightiest people in the land,' he said, 'yet none of you is free of guilt. None of you is capable of planting the apple seed. Yet I, who stole a piece of bread because I was starving, am condemned to death.'

And the king pardoned the wise thief.

Source unknown

31

The Stolen Smell

There was once a poor man who lived in the woods, and he had to forage every day for something to eat. The woods bordered on a rather beautiful town, and when the sun shone, and when he had the strength and energy, the poor man from the woods would walk into the town, and wander up and down the streets.

One particularly lovely morning, he was walking along the main street, gazing into the shop windows and enjoying the pleasure of simply being alive.

All at once, he caught a wonderful smell on the morning air. It was the smell of freshly baked bread, and it was coming from a baker's shop. Eagerly, he followed his nose, until he found himself inside the baker's shop, where the people of the town were buying their morning bread and their cakes for afternoon tea.

It wasn't that he envied them their feast. He simply wanted to breathe in great gulps of the lovely warm smell. That would be enough for him. The memory of it would keep him going all week. So he stood there, just inside the door, breathing deeply and savouring the rich aroma, filling his whole being with the wonder of it.

The baker watched him standing there, in his rags, inside the bakery door. And he didn't like what he saw. 'This man will put my customers off,' he thought, 'standing there breathing in the smell, and never thinking of buying anything. I can't let him get away with this.'

And so the baker called the policeman and had the man arrested because, he claimed, 'This man has been stealing my smells!' The policeman took the poor man away, and brought him to the courthouse. When the time for the trial came up, the judge called the poor man and the baker into the courtroom, and listened to their stories.

'This man stole my smells,' the baker claimed.

'I only breathed,' the poor man defended himself. 'See, I took nothing away from the shop. You can't steal a smell.'

The judge carefully weighed up all the evidence, and in due course he delivered his verdict. 'I find the poor man guilty of stealing the baker's smells,' he declared, 'and this court demands that the prisoner shall pay the baker recompense of one hundred pounds.'

The poor man gasped in disbelief. 'How will I ever get a hundred pounds?' he asked. 'Have mercy on me. All I possess are these few pennies.' And he produced two tiny coins from the depths of his pocket.

'Bring me what you have,' the judge demanded. And the poor man despairingly brought the judge his last two pennies.

The judge took the pennies, and called the baker forwards. He held out the coins, and the baker made to seize them. The judge stopped him. 'Just have a good long look at them,' he told the baker. The baker stared at the coins. And the judge duly returned them to the poor man, who put them back in his pocket.

'The poor man stole your smells,' the judge concluded, 'and now you have been paid in kind. The case is closed.'

Retelling of a Northumbrian community story

32

The Window

Two men, both seriously ill, were in the same ward of a great hospital. It was quite a small ward, with just room for the pair of them... a door opening on the corridor, and one window looking out on the world.

Now, one of the men was allowed to sit up for an hour in the morning and an hour in the afternoon, and his bed was next to the window. But the other man had to spend all his time flat on his back. And both of them had to be kept quiet and still. Of course, one of the disadvantages of their condition was that they were not allowed to do much: no reading, no radio, no television... they just had to keep quiet and still... just the two of them. Well, they used to talk for hours and hours... about their wives and children, their homes, their jobs, what they did during the war, where they'd been on holidays... all that sort of thing. And every morning and afternoon, when the man in the bed next to the window was propped up for his hour, he would describe what he could see outside. And the other man almost began to live for these hours.

The window apparently overlooked a park, with a lake, and there were the usual ducks and swans, children throwing them bread and sailing model yachts, young lovers walking hand in hand beneath the trees. And there were flowers, mainly roses, but with a magnificent border of dahlias and marigolds – bronze and gold and crimson. In the far corner was a tennis court, and at times the games were really good. And there was cricket, not quite up to Test Match standard, but better than nothing. And there was a bowling green, and right at the back, a row of shops with a view of the city behind.

And the man on his back would listen to all of this, enjoying every minute... how a child nearly fell into the lake, how beautiful the girls were in their summer dresses, and then an exciting tennis match. And he got so that he could almost see what was happening out there.

Then one afternoon, when a batsman was knocking some slow bowling all over the cricket ground, the thought struck him: why should the man next to the window have all the pleasure of seeing what was going on? Why shouldn't he get that chance? He felt ashamed, and tried not to think like that, but the more he tried the worse it became… Until, in a few days, it all turned sour: why wasn't *he* near the window?

And he brooded by day and stayed awake by night, and grew even more seriously ill, with none of the doctors understanding why.

Then one night, as he stared at the ceiling, the other man suddenly woke up, coughing and choking, the fluid congesting in his lungs, his hands groping for the button that would bring the night nurse running.

But the man watched without moving. What had he ever done to deserve to have a bed by the window? The coughing racked the darkness… on and on… choking off… Then stopped… the sound of breathing stopped. And the other man continued to stare at the ceiling.

In the morning, the nurses came with water for their wash. They found the other man dead, and took away his body, quietly, with no fuss.

As soon as it seemed decent, the man asked if he could be moved to the bed next to the window. And they moved him, tucked him in, and made him quite comfortable… and left him alone to be quiet and still.

The minute they'd gone, he levered himself up on one elbow, painfully and laboriously, gasping… and looked out of the window.

It faced a blank wall!

Source unknown

The Two Brothers

They told me the story of two monks who were blood brothers. The younger one had offended the older, and the older just could not forgive him. Every morning, the younger one would knock on the door of his brother and call out, 'Forgive me, brother.' But he would not. Day after day this went on, year after year.

After many years, the younger brother did not show up one morning. Nor the next, nor the next. The older one became uneasy. Finally, he went out to look for his brother. He knocked on every door. 'Have you seen my brother?' No one had. He left the monastery, knocked on the doors of all the neighbours. 'Have you seen my brother?'

He kept going. Miles away from the monastery he would knock on a door. 'Have you seen my brother?' People thought him strange, but he kept it up. Days went by, months, years. And that was all he had to say, except that when someone would show annoyance he would say, 'Forgive me, brother.'

At last, after so many years of searching, he found himself back at his monastery. He knocked. The young brother who answered did not recognize him, but he was struck by the beauty of his face. He ran to call the others. They all came, crowding around. They were all struck by the beauty of this old man. Now some of the older ones recognized him. When they called out his name, he fell on his face. 'Forgive me, brothers,' he said.

They wept, all of them.

Well, they made up a cell for him right beside the abbot's cell. And now, whenever any monk has difficulty forgiving his brother, why, he just slips in there for a few minutes.

Theophane the Monk

The Two Champions

There were two kingdoms that shared a common border. In one country they worshipped the sun, and in the other they worshipped the moon. Because of their religious differences, the two kingdoms went to war. Each gathered an army and the two armies met at the frontier. Row upon row of warriors, sunlight glinting on their war gear, faced each other across the no man's land.

It was agreed that each army should send forward a champion to fight in single combat. The strongest, most skilful warrior in each army was selected. The two men advanced towards each other, grim faced, with a sword in one hand and a shield in the other. On the chest of one was emblazoned an image of the sun; on the chest of the other, an image of the moon.

When they met, they fought like demons. They fought all morning long, as the sun rose higher in the sky. They fought through the midday heat, when the sun was at the zenith. They fought on and on as the sun descended towards the west. They were both such strong and skilful fighters that neither man could gain the advantage. They were still fighting, nose to nose, locked in each other's arms, when at last the sun went down. But by then they were exhausted. They both collapsed on the ground, too feeble even to crawl back to the camps their respective armies had made for the night.

'I hate you!' groaned the Champion of the Sun.

'I hate you!' replied the Champion of the Moon.

'I have to kill you,' said the Champion of the Sun. 'Back home I have a wife who loves me and a little boy who wants to be a warrior like me. I have to protect them from the likes of you.'

'I had a wife,' said the Champion of the Moon. 'Your people killed her in the last war. That's why I have to kill you.'

The moon rose. Presently, the Champion of the Sun asked the other man, 'What was she like, your wife?'

'She was lovely. We'd been sweethearts since we were children. I used to play with her in the woods near here.'

'Sounds like you had a happy childhood,' said the Champion of the Sun. 'Not like mine. My father made us work all day in the fields and he'd beat us if we complained.'

'I'm sorry to hear that,' said the Champion of the Moon.

And so they talked about their childhoods and the other things they had done in their lives. They talked and talked as the moon rose higher in the sky. Still they talked as the moon descended towards the west. Only for the last hour or two of the night did they sleep. Side by side they lay, their swords and shields dumped beside them.

The sky turned grey, then pink in the east. Sounds and smells of breakfast-making emanated from the two camps. The two sleeping champions were woken by the warmth of sunshine on their faces. Wearily, painfully, they creaked to their feet. They looked into each other's eyes. Then they embraced, and, leaving their swords and shields behind, walked back to their respective armies.

They could not fight each other any more, for you cannot fight someone when you know their story.

Retelling by Anthony Nanson

35

(A)LO13

Judgment

A story is told about an incident that happened during the thirties in New York, on one of the coldest days of the year. The world was in the grip of the Great Depression, and all over the city, the poor were close to starvation.

It happened that the judge was sitting on the bench that day, hearing a complaint against a woman who was charged with stealing a loaf of bread. She pleaded that her daughter was sick, and her grandchildren were starving, because their father had abandoned the family. But the shopkeeper, whose loaf had been stolen, refused to drop the charge. He insisted that an example be made of the poor old woman, as a deterrent to others.

The judge sighed. He was most reluctant to pass judgment on the woman, yet he had no alternative. 'I'm sorry,' he turned to her. 'But I can't make any exceptions. The law is the law. I sentence you to a fine of ten dollars, and if you can't pay I must send you to jail for ten days.'

The woman was heartbroken, but even as he was passing sentence, the judge was reaching into his pocket for the money to pay off the ten-dollar fine. He took off his hat, tossed the ten-dollar bill into it, and then addressed the crowd: 'I am also going to impose a fine of fifty cents on every person here present in this courtroom, for living in a town where a person has to steal bread to save her grandchildren from starvation. Please collect the fines, Mr Bailiff, in this hat, and pass them across to the defendant.'

And so the accused went home that day from the courtroom with forty-seven dollars and fifty cents – fifty cents of which had been paid by the shame-faced grocery store keeper who had brought the charge against her. And as she left the courtroom, the gathering of petty criminals and New York policemen gave the judge a standing ovation.

Based on an incident reported by James N. McCutcheon

36

The Auction

There was once a wealthy man who owned a priceless art collection, including a number of old masters that were the envy of many art connoisseurs. This same man also had a much-loved son, and they often used to enjoy their art treasures together.

However, war broke out, and the son was called up, and went off to fight. One day, the telegram arrived informing the father that his son had been killed in action. The old man was devastated. He grieved silently, alone and unremittingly.

A few months went by, and one day there was a knock at the door. A young man stood there, with a small package under his arm. 'You don't know me,' he introduced himself, 'but I knew your son very well. We were in the same unit, and I was with him when he died. I am the soldier he gave his life for. He saved many lives that day, and he was carrying me to safety when the bullet struck him. We had become close friends, and before he died, I drew this little picture of him. I'm not a great artist, but I want you to have this sketch now.'

The father was silent for a long time, gazing into the eyes of his son, looking out from the soldier's sketch, his own eyes filling with tears as he gazed. Then he thanked the soldier and offered to pay for the picture.

'Oh no, sir. It's a gift. I can never repay what your son did for me, but I want you to have this sketch. It's all I have to give.'

The father hung the portrait above the mantelpiece for everyone to see. He treasured it far more than all his other paintings put together, and he showed visitors the portrait of his son before he took them to visit any other paintings.

Not long after this incident, the old man died himself, and his art collection was put up for auction. Art collectors came from all over the world, thrilled at the possibility of buying one of the treasures. The auctioneer began the bidding. The first picture to come up for auction was the unknown soldier's sketch of the father's son. The auctioneer tried to start the bidding.

'What am I bid for this first picture in the collection?' he asked.

There was silence. Then there were rumblings and grumblings. 'Come on,' the art collectors said, 'get on with the real stuff. No one's interested in that old sketch. We've come for the valuable pieces. Why don't you just get on with the sale?'

But the auctioneer was having none of it. 'I'm sorry,' he said, 'but my instructions are clear. The deceased insists that the first item in the sale is this picture of the son. Now who will start me off with ten pounds for the son?'

Tentatively, a hand was raised at the back of the auction room. It was the gardener. He had worked for years for the old man, and he had loved the son. 'I'll give you ten pounds for the son,' he said. It was all he could afford. The hammer went down: once, twice, three times. No further bids. No one else was at all interested.

'Sold!' called the auctioneer. 'To the man at the back, for ten pounds!' There was relief all round. Now the buyers could get their hands on the valuable pieces. But the auctioneer laid down his gavel. 'The auction is over,' he declared. 'My instructions from the deceased are that whoever takes the son receives the entire estate, including the whole art collection. The man at the back who took the son receives everything.'

Source unknown

Lasting Values

37

The Fisherman's Dream

A fisherman once sat in the midday sun, gazing out to sea, watching his little fishing boat riding at anchor, and thinking to himself how good it was to sit in the sun with no worries, watch the waves breaking and enjoy God's creation.

But his daydream was interrupted when a smartly dressed and rather overweight businessman came up to him and broke into his reverie with a sharp question: 'What are you doing lazing around at midday? Why aren't you out fishing?'

Somewhat taken aback, the fisherman replied, 'I've done my day's fishing. I've taken my fish to market, and now I'm relaxing in the sun.'

'But why don't you put out to sea again and catch some more fish?' his questioner insisted.

'Why would I want to do that?' replied the fisherman politely.

'Well, then you would make twice as much money.'

'Why would I want to do that?'

'Well, then you could buy a bigger, better boat, and catch even more fish. You could even employ other people to do the fishing. My word, you could own a whole fleet of fishing boats if you weren't so lazy.'

'Why would I want to do that?'

'Well, if you owned your own fleet of boats, and employed other people to do the fishing, you would have as much money as you could ever dream of.'

'Why would I want that?'

'Well, then you could spend the rest of your life just doing whatever you wanted to do, sitting in the sun, relaxing and enjoying yourself, with no worries…'

Source unknown

38

Letting Go

There was once a really old man, who had lived a long and very happy life on a beautiful island. He loved his homeland greatly. There on his island, all his family, through all the generations, had lived, made their homes and earned their daily bread. And so, when the old man realized that he was approaching the last days of his life, he asked his sons to take him outside one last time. There, he knelt and gathered a handful of his native soil, and clutched it tightly in his gnarled old fingers.

Soon afterwards, the old man died and came to the gates of heaven. The angels greeted him joyfully. 'You have lived a good life,' they exclaimed. 'Welcome to the kingdom of heaven. Please come in.'

So the old man tried to cross the threshold of the heavenly kingdom, but as he did so, a kindly angel said, 'You must let go of the soil you are clutching.'

'Oh no, I could never do that,' he cried. 'This is my native soil, the earth of my beloved island home.'

The angels were sad as they went back to heaven, leaving the old man wandering, lonely, outside the gates.

Many years passed, and the angels came again. They brought the old man a taste of the heavenly banquet and feasted with him there, outside the gates, trying to persuade him to come into the fullness of the kingdom. He wanted so much to join them for all eternity, but again, when they asked him to let go of the soil he was clutching, he couldn't bring himself to do so. And again, they had to leave him standing there, alone.

Finally, after many more years had passed, the angels came again, and this time they brought with them the old man's granddaughter, who had grown old in the meantime and had died herself. She was delighted to see her beloved grandfather standing there. 'Oh Grandad,' she cried, 'I'm so happy you are here. Please come and join us in the heavenly kingdom. We love you so much, and we want you with us for all eternity.' The old man was overwhelmed to see his little granddaughter there, and in his joy he flung out his arms to embrace her. And as he did so, the soil slipped right through his fingers.

With great joy, the angels now led him into his heavenly home, and the first thing he saw there was the whole of his beloved island, waiting there to greet him.

Retelling of a traditional Mediterranean story

39

The Chief's Three Sons

Once there was a Native American chief who was nearing the end of his life. Even though he had tried many times, he was not able to decide which of his sons should succeed him as chief.

One day, he gathered his sons together and told them, 'Do you see that mountain in the distance? I want you to journey to that mountain, climb to its summit and bring back the thing you think will be most helpful in leading our people.'

After several days, the first son returned with a load of flint stones, used to make arrow tips and spear points. He told his father, 'Our people will never live in fear of their enemies. I know where there is a mound of flint.'

The second son climbed to the top of the mountain, and on the way found forests rich with wood for making fires. When he returned, he said to his father, 'Our people will never be cold in winter. I know where wood can be found in abundance to keep them warm and to cook their food.'

The third son returned late and empty-handed. He stated, 'When I got to the summit, I found nothing worth bringing back. I searched everywhere, but the top of the mountain was barren rock and useless. Then I looked out towards the horizon, far into the distance. I was astonished to see new land filled with forests and meadows, mountains and valleys, fish and animals – a land of great beauty and great peace. I brought nothing back, for the land was still far off and I didn't have time to travel there. But I would love to go there someday; I delayed coming back because I found it very difficult to return after seeing the beauty of that land.'

The old chief's eyes blazed. He grasped his third son in his arms, proclaiming that he would succeed him as the new chief. He thought to himself, 'The other sons brought back worthy things, necessary things. But my third son has a vision. He has seen a better land, the promised land, and he burns with the desire to go there.'

Source unknown

Signs of Daybreak

A rabbi once asked his students how they could tell when night had ended and day was on its way back.

'Is it when you can see an animal in the distance, and can tell whether it is a sheep or a dog?'

'No,' answered the rabbi.

'Is it when you can look at a tree in the distance, and tell whether it is a fig tree or a peach tree?'

'No.'

'Well then,' the students demanded, 'when is it?'

'It is when you look on the face of another human being, and see that he or she is your brother or sister. Because if you cannot do that, then no matter what time it is, it is still night.'

Source unknown

A Goat Too Many

A poor man had come to the end of his tether, and he went to his rabbi for advice. 'Holy rabbi,' he cried, 'things are in a bad way at home, and getting worse. We are so poor, and we all live in a small hut – my wife and I, our in-laws and our six children. We are continually getting on each other's nerves, and we are always quarrelling. I can't carry on living like this!'

The rabbi thought hard for a moment, then he looked up. 'Do as I tell you,' he said, 'and things will soon get better. Tell me, what animals do you own?'

'I have a cow, a goat and some chickens.'

'Right, go home now and take all these animals into the hut to live with you.'

The man was dumbfounded, but he did as the rabbi had suggested. He brought all the animals into his house.

The next day, he went back to the rabbi. 'Rabbi,' he said, 'things are far worse than they were before. Our life is hell. Our home is like a barn. Please help me.'

'My son,' said the rabbi, 'go home and take the chickens out of your house. God will help you.'

So the poor man went home and took the chickens out of his house, and the next day he went back to the rabbi.

'Things are a bit better,' he admitted, 'but I still have a problem. The goat is smashing everything up. She is turning our life into a nightmare. Please help me.'

'Go home,' advised the rabbi, 'and take the goat out of the house. God will help you.'

So the poor man went home and took the goat out of the house. The next day, he was back with the rabbi again.

'That's a lot better,' he said, 'but the cow has turned our home into a stable. There's no way we can keep the house clean with a cow in the room all the time. Please help me.'

'You're right,' agreed the rabbi. 'I think you should go home and take the cow out of the house.'

So the poor man hurried home and took the cow out of the house. The next day, he came back to the rabbi.

'I don't know how to thank you,' he said. 'Your advice has really helped us. Now that we have all the animals out of the house, our home is quiet and clean again, with plenty of space, and life is sweet again. God has helped me indeed.'

Retelling of a traditional story

42

The Emperor's Gift

There was once a poor, penniless beggar, who sat in the streets of an Indian town, day after day, begging passers-by for a little rice. At night, he would sleep on his mat, with only a few old rags to protect him against the cold night air.

Most days, he would be given enough rice to make himself a small meal at night, and enough coppers to buy a little firewood, to cook the rice. And so his life continued, day after day – until one day, he heard that the emperor was coming to the town to make a state visit.

'Surely,' he thought, 'the emperor is a good and saintly man. He will give me good gifts. He will not pass me by with a mere handful of rice.' So the next day, he made sure that he was sitting on the route where the emperor was going to pass by.

Soon, the sound of the imperial procession was heard, and the beggar placed himself beside the road. As the emperor's coach approached, he was about to step out and beg for alms, when to his great surprise, the emperor himself got out of his coach, came up to the beggar, greeted him warmly and humbly, and asked the beggar for a little gift of rice.

The beggar was shocked and deeply disappointed. He, after all, was the poor man, struggling to survive and dependent on the gifts of others, yet here was the rich and powerful emperor begging a little rice from the poorest of the poor. He could scarcely conceal his indignation. Yet he could scarcely refuse the emperor's request either, so very reluctantly he counted out five grains of rice from the meagre supply in his bowl and gave them to the emperor, who received them graciously, thanked the beggar warmly and went on his way.

That night, the beggar began to prepare his meal. As he cleaned the rice, he noticed something shining in among the grains. Yes, there was a nugget of gold among the rice. And another. And another. He sifted through the rice with the utmost care, and to his amazement he discovered five nuggets of gold. Five. And no more.

He thought back to his encounter with the emperor. For each of the five grains of rice he had so reluctantly given to the emperor, he now had a nugget of gold. The emperor had returned his grudging gift with its equivalent in gold.

'How mean and foolish I have been,' he said to himself. 'How I wish I had given the emperor every last grain of rice I possessed!'

Retelling of a traditional Indian story

43

The Student Santa

The students were having their briefing about how to be a good 'Santa Claus'. The Christmas season was gearing up in the department store, and Alex was here on his first day as a 'holiday-job Santa'.

'Whatever you do, don't frighten the children,' the manager told them sternly. 'Not even if the parents want you to!'

Armed with this advice, Alex started his first day. The very first child that arrived, parents in tow, screamed blue murder the moment he set eyes on Alex's fine new Santa outfit and long white beard. Nothing would pacify him. Not the parents' admonitions to 'be a brave boy', and not Alex's own attempts to console the crying child.

Eventually, in despair, Alex hit on an idea. He began to peel off his 'uniform' bit by bit, starting with the white beard. The child stopped crying, and watched him, fascinated. The red hood was removed, and a young and rather embarrassed face came to light. The glasses were removed, and two twinkling, youthful, blue eyes appeared. The red robe was discarded, and underneath it was an ordinary lad in jeans and a sweatshirt. The child looked on in amazement, until he was soon laughing and relaxed.

Once the relationship between them had been established, Alex started to put the 'uniform' back on again, and as he did so, he told the little boy a story of how, a very long time ago, God himself had come down to live on earth with us, and so that no one would be frightened by him, he had come in very ordinary clothes and lived the life of a very ordinary child. The boy listened, wide-eyed.

Soon, it was time to move on. The next 'customer' was waiting. The boy's parents moved away, rather disgruntled. 'What a shame,' they said. 'It's spoiled all the magic.'

'The end of the magic, perhaps,' mused Alex, 'but the beginning of the wonder.'

Source unknown

The Story of Two Sons

A king had two sons. As he grew older, he wanted to pass on the kingdom to one of these two sons and make him his heir. He assembled all the wise men and women of the land, and called his two sons to present themselves. He gave each of them five pieces of silver and told them: 'By evening, I want you to have filled up this whole hall. What you fill it up with is up to you. You can use the silver pieces if you have to.'

And the wise folk said, 'This is a good task.'

The older son went off, and came to a field where the farm labourers were harvesting sugar beet and putting it through a press. The remainder, after pressing, was discarded. So the older son made an arrangement with the foreman of the labourers, to take all the discarded sugar beet and fill up the hall with it. When the task was complete, he gave the foreman the five pieces of silver, and told his father that the task was done. There would be no need for his younger brother to try. He had filled the hall. But his father replied, 'There is still time. We will wait.'

The younger son came back, and asked for the sugar beet remains to be moved out of the hall again. He had nothing in his hands but a candle. When the hall was completely empty once more, he carried this candle into the middle of the hall and lit it. Immediately, the whole hall was filled with light. Light streamed into every remote corner.

And the king said to the younger son, 'You shall be my heir. Your brother has spent five pieces of silver to fill up the hall with useless rubbish. You haven't used even a single piece of silver, yet you have filled the hall with light. You have filled it with the very thing that my people need above all else.'

Retelling of a traditional Philippine story

The Water of Life

Three people were searching for the water of life, hoping to drink from it and live forever.

The first was a warrior: he reckoned the water of life would be very mighty – a torrent or a rapid – so he went in full armour, with all his weapons, believing he could force the water to yield to him.

The second was an enchantress: she reckoned the water of life would be very magical – perhaps a whirlpool or a geyser, something she would need to manipulate with spells – so she went in her long star-spangled robe, hoping to outwit the water.

The third was a trader: he reckoned the water of life would be very costly – a fountain of pearl-drops or diamonds, perhaps – so he loaded his clothes and purses with money, hoping to be able to buy the water.

When the travellers reached their destination, they found they had all been quite wrong about the water of life.

It wasn't a torrent to be intimidated by force.

It wasn't a whirlpool to be charmed by spells.

And it wasn't a fountain of pearl-drops or diamonds to be bought for money.

It was just a tiny, sparkling spring; its benefits were absolutely free – but, of course, you had to kneel to drink from it.

This caused the seekers great consternation.

The warrior was in full armour and couldn't bend.

The enchantress had on her long magic robe, and if that became soiled it would lose its power.

The trader was so loaded with money that if he did no more than incline his head, coins would start rolling away into corners and crevices.

All dressed up, the three could not lower themselves to drink from the spring of the water of life.

There was only one solution.

So the warrior laid aside his armour.

The enchantress laid aside her magic robe.

And the trader laid aside the clothes he had stuffed with money.

And then each of them – naked – could kneel to drink from the water of life and receive its sweet, cool, startling benefits.

Kate Compston

46

The Guest's Speech

It was a special occasion in the life of the church. The community had been in that place for two hundred years, and the church was celebrating its special anniversary in grand style.

The congregation had prepared a great feast, and everyone in the neighbourhood was invited to come along. The pastor welcomed them all, and invited them to enjoy the party. He was a good man, and everyone loved him, whether they went to church or not. Everyone recognized the man's humility and godliness, and respected him deeply.

When the feasting was over, the entertainment began. The pastor had invited a well-known television personality along, to make a speech. The crowd waited, expectantly, to hear what this famous and popular actor would say. To their surprise, he began by reciting the familiar words of Psalm 23, 'The Lord is my shepherd'.

Everyone sat quietly, very moved by the actor's rendering of their favourite psalm, and when he finished, they applauded him with great enthusiasm. But he had not quite finished. As the applause died away, he turned to the pastor and asked him to recite the same psalm himself, for the people.

The pastor was embarrassed. 'Oh dear,' he stuttered, 'it will sound so weak and feeble after your fine rendering. I'm not a public speaker. The folk will laugh at me, after hearing you.' But the actor insisted, and reluctantly the pastor rose to his feet and began to recite the psalm.

The people fell silent as the familiar words carried through the night air. The pastor clearly forgot where he was and what he was doing as he put his heart and soul into the recitation of the beloved psalm. When he came to the end, there was a stunned silence for a few seconds, and many of the people had tears in their eyes and a lump in their throats. And only after this sacred space of wonder did they respond with tumultuous applause.

The pastor sat down and the actor addressed them again.

'You see, my friends,' he told them, 'I know the psalm. But this man here – he knows the shepherd!'

Retelling of a traditional story

Warnings

47

The Abandoned City

In a land across the sea, there is an old city where no one lives. Weeds grow on the rooftops of ruined houses and the streets are overgrown with grass and nettles. But once, it was a thriving township.

Long ago, hundreds of people lived here. One afternoon, a wise and holy man was seen walking along the main street. His eyes were full of tears. He kept his head bowed low as he made his way through the town centre and out to the open countryside. The townspeople watched him, shocked. But no one dared to ask him the reason for his obvious distress.

Then the mayor made a guess. 'Someone must have died at the other side of town,' he suggested.

A woman took up the story. 'Could it be the plague?' she asked. A young woman began to weep, as she thought of how the plague might kill her little children. In no time, the town was in uproar, quite certain that the plague had struck. There was a frantic scramble to get away from the town before the infection spread. The people loaded up their donkeys and carts, and streamed out into the countryside. Within an hour, there was not a single soul remaining in the town.

Later that day, the holy man came back to his house. He couldn't begin to understand the emptiness that he discovered. After all, only a short while before, he had been happily peeling onions for his dinner, and he had only gone out for a while to give his streaming eyes a little rest.

Retelling of a traditional story

48

The Investment

There once lived a rich man who had no greater desire than to do good to those around him, and especially to those who worked for him.

He noticed that one of his workmen, a carpenter, was very poor and was struggling to feed his family. He could see for himself that the hovel in which the man lived with his wife and children was falling into disrepair, and was no longer a match for the cold and the rain that beat down upon it. He felt great compassion for the carpenter and his family, and he had an idea.

He called the carpenter to him one morning and gave him these instructions: 'I want you to build me a beautiful house,' he said. 'I want you to spare no expense, and to employ only the very best craftsmen for every job that is needed. I have to make a journey, and I will be away for a while, but when I come back, I want you to have the house ready for me.'

The carpenter was delighted to be given this task. Immediately, he set to work, and, knowing that the master would be away, he decided to make a good profit on this enterprise. Instead of hiring the best craftsmen and using the finest materials, he cut corners wherever he possibly could. The master would never know, and he could keep the difference and make a lot of money for himself.

And so the house was built. From the outside, it looked beautiful, but as the carpenter well knew, it was not at all sound. The timbers in the roof were weak and badly fitted. The bricks were seconds, which would soon begin to crumble. The roof tiles were rejects from the quarry. The building had been carried out by inexperienced workers for low pay.

When the master returned, he came to inspect the house. 'I have done as you instructed,' the carpenter told him. 'I have used the best materials and the finest craftsmen.'

'I'm delighted to hear it,' said the master. 'Here are the keys. The house is yours. It is my gift to you and your family. May it be a fine home for you for the rest of your life.'

And in the years that followed, the carpenter could often be heard to mutter, under his breath, 'If only I had known that the house was meant for me…'

Retelling of a traditional story

Crutches

When an accident deprived the village headman of the use of his legs, he took to walking on crutches. He gradually developed the ability to move with speed – even to dance and execute little pirouettes for the entertainment of his neighbours.

Then he took it into his head to train his children in the use of crutches. It soon became a status symbol in the village to walk on crutches, and before long everyone was doing so.

By the fourth generation, no one in the village could walk without crutches. The village school included 'Crutchery: theoretical and applied' in its curriculum, and the village craftsmen became famous for the quality of the crutches they produced. There was even talk of developing an electronic, battery-operated set of crutches!

One day, a young Turk presented himself before the village elders, and demanded to know why everyone had to walk on crutches, since God had provided people with legs to walk on. The village elders were amused that this upstart should think himself wiser than they, so they decided to teach him a lesson. 'Why don't you show us how?' they said.

'Agreed,' cried the young man.

A demonstration was fixed for the following Sunday at the village square. Everyone was there when the young man hobbled on his crutches to the middle of the square, stood upright, and dropped his crutches. A hush fell on the crowd as he took a bold step forwards – and fell flat on his face.

With that, everyone was confirmed in their belief that it was quite impossible to walk without the help of crutches.

Anthony de Mello

The Dancing Crane

There was once a very poor student. He was a very clever young man, a poet and a very gifted artist, but he never had two pennies to rub together. He had a friend who owned a pub, and often in the evenings he would go along to this pub and sit by the fire, drawing, writing and drinking cups of tea, and his friend would give him something to eat.

One night, the student came to the pub as usual, but this time he didn't sit down in his usual corner. Instead, he took some chalk and began to draw a picture of a crane on the wall. All the guests and the landlord himself watched, fascinated as the details of this magnificent bird started to take shape, half expecting it to spread its wings any minute and fly away.

When he had finished, the student turned to the innkeeper and said, 'You've been so kind to me all this time, letting me sit here drawing, and giving me cups of tea. I'd like to repay you. So I have drawn this crane for you. It's a magic crane. If you clap your hands three times, it will stand up and dance for you. But it will only do this once a day. If you try to make it dance more than this, it will go away and you will never see it again.'

And with these words, the student clapped his hands, and indeed the crane stood up gracefully and performed an intricate dance. The guests were astounded, and watched as the bird completed its dance and once more became a motionless picture on the wall.

Well, as you can imagine, trade was booming in the pub after that. Everyone wanted to see the dancing crane. But the innkeeper always heeded the student's warning, and never asked the crane to dance more than once a day.

One night, however, a local millionaire came into the pub – a mean and cruel man, whom no one liked or trusted. He had heard about the dancing crane, and insisted on seeing it in action. Now the bird had already danced once that day, and the innkeeper was adamant, but the rich man was insistent and threw a bag of gold on the table. 'I want to see it dance,' he roared, 'and I'm not leaving here until I have!'

What could the poor innkeeper do? Very reluctantly, he clapped his hands three times. The crane stood up, very slowly, its head hanging. It danced that night, but what a sorrowful dance it was, and everyone who saw it was in tears. When the dance was over, the door opened and the poor student came in. Without a word, he picked up the dying crane, tucked it underneath his arm, and walked away into the night. Neither the crane nor the student was ever seen again.

Retelling of a Chinese folk story

51

The Devil's Apprentices

It was the start of a new term in hell, and the devil was giving an induction course to the latest batch of apprentices.

'There's no room for complacency,' he warned them. 'You wouldn't believe the half of what is going on down on earth. People are getting more and more in touch with God. They are starting to see God in creation, and even in each other's hearts. They are noticing God's action in the stories of their own lives. And worse than that, they are starting to realize how important it is to work for justice and for peace. If things carry on like this, God's kingdom will come, and we'll all be out of a job.'

There was a long silence, as the seriousness of the devil's message sank in. The apprentices waited to hear what wisdom the devil would give them for dealing with this perilous situation down on earth. But he could read the questions in their minds, and he turned the whole problem over to them.

'So what are you going to do about it?' he asked them. 'Any bright ideas?'

They scratched their heads and furrowed their brows.

'Come on,' urged the devil. 'I'm waiting. We don't have forever, you know!'

Very tentatively, the first apprentice raised his arm. 'Sir,' he ventured, 'why don't we go down and tell them there's no God?'

'Sorry to disappoint you,' the devil said. 'But that wouldn't wash at all. They seem to be born with something deep in their hearts that attracts them back to God. They often can't name it, or even admit that it is there, but sooner or later they all have a moment when they know that God exists. You'll have to come up with a better idea than that.'

Crestfallen, the first apprentice sat down, and the second apprentice raised his arm.

'Sir,' he suggested, 'could we perhaps go down there and tell them that there is no such thing as sin, and so they have nothing to fear. Hell is just a myth?'

'A good try,' said the devil, 'but unfortunately, the same bit of God that is deep in their hearts also tells them when they are going off course. They know – if they stop to listen to that inner voice – that it is all too possible to commit sin, and they know that when they do, they can feel so terrible afterwards, until they have put things right again. Deep in their hearts, they know what sin is and how "hell" feels. Think again. What about you?' he said, turning to the third apprentice. 'What have you got to say for yourself?'

'Well,' replied the third apprentice, slowly and thoughtfully. 'I've been giving it a lot of thought. You say that it's no good us telling them that there is no God. And it's no use our telling them that there is no sin. How would it be if we told them that there is no hurry?'

The devil was delighted. 'Brilliant!' he squealed. 'That's exactly what we'll do. You'll go far, young demon. Well done.'

And so it came to be that the human race carried on believing in God and knowing about sin, but never doing much about it, because, after all, there was no hurry.

Source unknown

The Ferocious Dog

There was once a perfectly normal little dog – neither fierce nor timid. One day, this little dog wandered off to a nearby fairground, and found itself inside the hall of mirrors.

The little dog took one look around, and saw hundreds of dogs staring back at it. Terrified at being so surrounded, it began to bark and to bare its teeth. To its horror, every one of the hundreds of other dogs did the same. Suddenly the ordinary little dog was in the midst of a hostile army of strange and fearsome looking animals. Its barking grew even more frantic and its growl more vicious. It tried to bite the other dogs, but as soon as it got near to them, they too growled and tried to bite.

This might have gone on all night, but the little dog's owner came looking for it. As soon as the little dog caught sight of its owner and heard the familiar call, it began to wag its tail and jump up and down for joy.

And yes, all the other dogs did the same. And the little dog went home thinking that perhaps the big wide world wasn't quite as terrifying as it had first thought.

Retelling of a traditional Indian story

The Legend of the Stones

Two women approached a wise man and asked for instruction. One of them regarded herself as a terrible sinner. In her youth, she had deceived her husband, and she tortured herself constantly with the memory of her infidelity.

The second, on the other hand, had lived her entire life within the law and by the rules. She wasn't conscious of any serious sin, had nothing much to reproach herself with and felt quite pleased with herself.

The wise man asked both women about their life. The first wept as she confessed her great sin. She felt that her sin had been so great that she had no right to expect forgiveness. The second said that she had not committed any particular sins.

The wise man said to the first woman, 'Go, daughter of God, and look for the heaviest boulder you can find – one that you can barely manage to carry – and bring it to me.'

'And you,' he said to the second woman, who could not recall any serious sin, 'go and bring me as many stones as you can carry, but they must all be small ones.'

The women went off to do as the wise man had told them. The first brought a huge boulder; the second brought a whole sackful of small pebbles.

The wise man examined the stones and said, 'Now do as follows. Take the stones back and replace each one of them exactly where you picked it up, and when you have put them all back where you found them, come back to me.'

The women went off again to carry out the wise man's instructions. The first very easily found the place from where she had taken the huge boulder, and she replaced it where it had been. But the second had no idea where she had picked up all her little pebbles, and had to return to the wise man without having carried out his instruction.

'You see,' said the wise man, 'that's how it is with our sins. It was easy to take the big, heavy boulder back to its place because you knew exactly where you first found it. But it was impossible to remember where all those little pebbles came from.'

And to the first woman, he said, 'You are very conscious of your sin. You carry in your heart the reproach of your husband and of your conscience; you have learned humility, and in this way you have been freed of the boulder of your wrongdoing. You, however,' he said to the second woman, who had come back still carrying her sack of little pebbles, 'you, who have sinned in many small ways, do not know any more when and how you did wrong; you are not able to repent. You have grown accustomed to a life of little sins, to passing judgment on the sins of others while becoming more deeply entangled in your own. It has become impossible to free yourself of them.'

Retelling of a story by Leo Tolstoy

54

The Firemaker

Once upon a time, there lived a man who was able to make fire. The people of his village were amazed at this wondrous gift. The first time he ever made fire, they didn't rightly know what to think of it, or what to do with it. In fact, if the truth were told, they were perhaps a little bit afraid of it.

But then the firemaker taught them how they could use this gift to keep warm through the cold of winter, and to make a warm, dancing light when the darkness wrapped its blanket around them every night. They could use it, he showed them, to cook their food, and even to fire their pottery, from which to eat their food. If ever they were alone and lost in the wilderness, they could use this gift to send up a cry for help, and their signal would be seen far away, and rescue would come.

Fire could be dangerous, however, and it could cause destruction. So the firemaker also taught them how to handle the fire reverently and with care, so that it should not cause hurt to themselves or to any part of creation.

In no time at all, the news of the firemaker's gift spread from one village to the next, until everyone in the region had heard about this mysterious and powerful gift. The firemaker was in great demand. He travelled through the villages, teaching his skills to everyone who wanted to learn. And the people learned eagerly, and they began to revere the firemaker. Surely this man was special, and the gods were very close to him.

In time, the popularity of the firemaker came to the attention of the village elders and rulers, and to the lord of that region. They didn't entirely like what they were hearing. Here was a man who appeared to be giving the people what they deeply desired, and what would give them fuller and happier lives. The people were turning away from their rulers and leaders to follow this upstart firemaker. The leaders and rulers were losing control!

The firemaker's activities had to be curbed, they all agreed. And when that didn't seem to be possible, they had to resort to sterner measures. The firemaker must go, they resolved. And so, one night, they trapped the firemaker in a dark corner and they killed him. They told the people that from then on, it would be illegal to make fires.

The people were dismayed, but most of them were too afraid to challenge the rulers. Instead, they grieved for the firemaker, whom they had all loved. They forgot most of what he had taught them, because they never practised their skills again, but they never forgot *him*.

The rulers and leaders conferred as to how to placate the people and take their minds off this dangerous man. They hit upon the idea of encouraging the people to build shrines to the memory of the firemaker. And so, in every village, a monument was erected. The people decorated these shrines with flowers, beautiful paintings and statues. They gathered together regularly there to remember the firemaker and all he had meant to them. They wrote down in books the instructions he had once given them about the fire, and they read extracts from these books every time they met together. The rulers were pleased, because they had brought the fire under control. But the people got used to chilly, dark nights again, and they ate cold food, and they forgot how to dance and sing in the firelight.

They remained faithful, for as long as history lasted, in paying homage at the shrines of the firemaker. But there was no fire.

Retelling of a traditional story

The Onion

There was once a peasant woman who was very wicked indeed. When she died, no one could recall a single good deed that she had left behind her. And so she fell into the hands of the devils, who plunged her into a lake of fire.

But her guardian angel hadn't given up on her, and stood pondering what he could do to save her. If he could discover just one good deed of hers and tell God about it, she might yet be saved.

And as he recalled the details of her life, her guardian angel remembered something. 'She once pulled up an onion from her garden and gave it to a beggar woman,' he told God triumphantly.

And God replied, 'Then you take that onion and hold it out to her in the fiery lake. Let her take hold of the onion and use it to pull her out. If you can pull her out of the lake, she can come to heaven, but if the onion breaks, she will have to stay where she is.'

The angel went straight off to the fiery lake and held out the onion to the despairing peasant woman. 'Catch hold of the onion,' he called to her, 'and hold on tightly, while I try to pull you out.'

The woman seized the onion eagerly, and the angel had almost managed to pull her out of the lake, when a crowd of other despairing souls saw what was happening and tried to catch hold of the woman, in the hope of being pulled out along with her.

As soon as she realized what was happening, she was furious, and she kicked out at the other sinners, to make them release their hold on her.

'It's *my* onion,' she cried. 'I'm the one to be pulled out – not you. You just stay where you are!'

And at these words, the onion broke. The woman fell back into the burning lake, and she is still there to this day. And the angel wept.

Retelling of a story by Fyodor Dostoevsky

The Otter's Children

The otter rushed before the king, crying aloud, 'My lord, you are a king who loves justice and rules fairly. You have established peace among all your creatures, and yet there is no peace.'

'Who has broken the peace?' demanded the king.

'The weasel!' shouted the otter. 'I dived into the water to hunt for food for my children, leaving them in the care of the weasel. While I was gone, my children were killed. "An eye for an eye", the good book says. I demand vengeance!'

The king sent for the weasel, who soon appeared before him. 'You have been charged with the death of the otter's children. How do you plead?' demanded the king.

'Alas, my lord,' wept the weasel, 'I am responsible for the death of the otter's children, though it was clearly an accident. As I heard the woodpecker sound the danger alarm, I rushed to defend our land. In doing so, I trampled the otter's children by accident.'

The king summoned the woodpecker. 'Is it true that you sounded the alarm with your mighty beak?' enquired the king.

'It is true, my lord,' replied the woodpecker. 'I began the alarm when I spied the scorpion sharpening its dagger.'

When the scorpion appeared before the king, it was asked if it indeed had sharpened its dagger.

'You understand that sharpening your dagger is an act of war?' declared the king.

'I understand,' replied the scorpion, 'but I prepared only because I observed the turtle polishing its armour.'

In its defence, the turtle said, 'I would not have polished my armour if I had not seen the crab preparing its sword.'

The crab declared, 'I saw the lobster swinging its javelin.'

When the lobster appeared before the king, it explained, 'I began to swing my javelin when I saw the otter swimming towards my children, ready to devour them.'

Turning to the otter, the king announced, 'You, not the weasel, are the guilty party. The blood of your children is upon your head. Whoever sows death shall reap it.'

Retelling of a Jewish folk story

57

The Soul-Taker

Three sisters lived in the hills. They were kind and generous people of deep faith. One day, they were digging in the backyard of their home when they uncovered a large box. They opened it up and discovered that it was full of gold. All three began to scream, 'Beware of the soul-taker! Whatever will we do? Do we bury it again, or do we simply leave our house?'

Four men who had recently moved into the house next door overheard the conversation. They walked to the home of the three sisters and enquired about their problem. 'We are trying to decide how to get away from the soul-taker,' they said.

'What is a soul-taker?' one of the men asked. 'Show us.'

The sisters walked to the far corner of their backyard and pointed to the box full of coins. 'This is the soul-taker,' they said.

The four men laughed. 'Can you believe it?' the large one asked. 'They think gold is a soul-taker.' The others roared with laughter.

The bearded one spoke next: 'If you women are frightened, go into town for a few hours and we'll take care of your problem.'

The women agreed and left immediately.

The four men began to make plans. They decided to divide the gold equally. They also decided that two of them would go to the store to get something to eat, and the other two would finish digging up the box.

The two men who had stayed to work agreed that things would be much better if they were able to split the gold two ways. They made plans to ambush and kill the other two when they returned, and to bury them in the hole where the box was found.

Meanwhile, the two men who had gone to buy food also decided to divide the gold between just the two of them. 'We'll poison the food,' they said. 'When the other two die, we'll bury them in the hole made by the box.'

When they returned from the store, the men who had stayed behind ambushed and killed their companions. Before they buried the corpses, they decide to eat the food while it was still fresh. Soon after they had begun to eat, they both grew very sick and died.

When the three sisters returned to their home, they saw four dead men and a box of gold. 'We told them that it was a soul-taker,' they said, 'but they didn't believe us.' And they left their home again to get away from the gold.

Retelling of an Armenian folk story

58

The Quail and the Hunter

A flock of quail once lived near a marsh. They flew every morning to the nearby fields to feed. However, there was one big problem with this arrangement. Near to the fields lived a bird hunter, who used to snare the quail and take them to market to be sold. He had become very proficient at this task, because he was able to imitate the call of the quail leader. When he imitated this call, all the quail thought that their leader was calling them, and they flocked into the hunter's net.

One day, the quail held a meeting, and listened as their leader spoke to them. 'We need to put a stop to this,' he warned them, 'or soon there won't be any of us left. I know how the hunter is doing it. He is imitating my call to lure you into his net. So next time you hear his call, fly to the fields and let him catch you in his net. But when the net comes down, all poke your heads through the holes in the net together at the same time, fly off with the net, up to the thorn bushes. The net will get tangled up in the thorn bushes, and you will be able to pull yourselves free of the netting and fly away.'

So this is what the quail did. Every time they heard the hunter's imitation call, they let him catch them, then flew off together, tangled the net up in the thorn bushes and pulled themselves free. The hunter became more and more frustrated. He was making no money in his trade any more, and his wife was getting very impatient with him. 'Don't worry, dear,' he reassured her. 'Just wait until the quail begin to quarrel.'

And sure enough, one day the hunter made his call, and the quail rose up and flew to the field. Just as they were landing, one quail accidentally bumped into another. 'I'm sorry,' he apologized. 'I didn't see you there.'

'What do you mean, you didn't see me?' the other remonstrated. 'Are you blind, you clumsy fool? Can't you look where you're going?'

'Well,' the first quail replied, 'if you're going to take that attitude... I said it was an accident!'

In no time, the quarrel had spread through the flock. The quail all took one side or the other, and very soon they were all going at each other like bitter enemies. There was chaos on the field. The hunter smiled as he threw his net over them. But they were far too engrossed in their quarrelling to remember the agreed procedure. 'We're trapped,' they called out.

'Let's fly this way!' said some.

'No,' said the others, 'that way is safer!'

'Why should we do what you want all the time?' the first group replied. 'You're always telling us what to do. We're sick of doing things your way!'

And while they were bickering among themselves, the hunter gathered the whole flock up in his net, took them to market and made a small fortune.

Source unknown

59

God's Hat

One day, God took a walk across the earth, disguised as an old tramp. He made his way through the fields, where a group of friends were working, and decided to have a little joke with them. He put on a hat that was red on one side, white on the other, green at the front and black at the back.

As the friends walked home to their village that night, they talked about the old tramp.

'Did you see that old man in the white hat walking through the fields?' asked the first.

The second replied, 'No, it was a red hat!'

'Don't tell me that,' retorted the first. 'It was definitely white!'

'No, it wasn't,' argued the second. 'I saw it with my own two eyes, and it was red!'

'You must be blind!' said the first.

'There's nothing wrong with my eyes,' snapped the second. 'It's you! You must be drunk!'

'You're both blind,' chimed in a third. 'That fellow's hat was green!'

'What's the matter with you all?' rejoined a fourth. 'It was a black hat. Anyone could see that! You were obviously half asleep when he walked past. What fools you all are!'

And so the argument continued, and before they knew what was happening to them, the group of friends had become a band of enemies.

And the strife continues. To this day, the descendants of those former friends still go on arguing. The White Hatters versus the Red Hatters, the Green Hatters versus the Black Hatters – each party believing that it knows, beyond any doubt, the colour of God's Hat.

As for God, he still walks the fields in disguise, saddened now. But the Mad Hatters are too fiercely embroiled in their arguments to notice.

Retelling of a West African fable

At the City Gates

Long ago, in a far-away town, an old woman used to sit at the city gates, watching the travellers passing through, and sometimes engaging them in conversation.

One night, when it was growing dark, a traveller came along, weary from a hard day's walk. 'Excuse me,' he said to the old woman, 'but I am looking for a place to rest, and I wonder, can you tell me what the people are like in this town?'

The woman smiled, and in reply she asked him a question of her own. 'You have had a long journey,' she commented, 'and you must be feeling weary. Where do you come from?'

A little surprised by her question, the traveller told her the name of his home town. 'Mychester,' he said.

The woman was interested. 'Oh,' she smiled, 'and what are the people like in Mychester?'

'Oh,' replied the traveller, 'you wouldn't believe how awful people are in Mychester. They don't care if you are hungry and thirsty. They wouldn't even pass the time of day with you. And if you ask for help they turn away, or deliberately send you the wrong way. They are rude and unfriendly in the extreme.'

'My word,' replied the old woman. 'Well, I'm afraid I have bad news for you. The people here in this town are very much like the people in Mychester. I don't think you would like them very much.'

The traveller was disappointed. 'Oh well,' he sighed. 'I guess I'll move on then.'

A short time passed, and soon another traveller arrived at the city gates. He saw the old woman sitting there, smiled and approached her. 'Excuse me,' he said, 'but I am looking for a place to rest, and I wonder, can you tell me what the people are like in this town?'

The woman smiled back at him, and again she asked a question of her own. 'You have had a long journey,' she commented, 'and you must be feeling weary. Where do you come from?'

'I come from Mychester,' he told her.

'And what are the people like in Mychester?' the woman continued.

'Oh, they are so kind,' the traveller replied. 'I like them a lot. They are always friendly, ready to help each other and generous to a fault.'

'Well,' the woman told him, 'I think you will find a warm welcome here in this city. The people here are very much like the people in Mychester.'

Source unknown

61

The Wolf in the Woods

In a village hidden far away on the edge of a dense forest in northern Europe, there lived a small, contented little community. There was no crime, and so no policemen. Nothing much ever happened there, so there were no newspapers. But a nightwatchman used to walk around the village every night, just to make sure that no danger was lurking.

Imagine the consternation, therefore, when one morning the villagers awoke to find the watchman lying in a pool of blood, his bones crushed and his body half eaten. 'A wolf!' the villagers cried. 'Surely this can only be the work of a wolf.'

They buried the nightwatchman, and weeks passed by. Eventually, the villagers became less vigilant. Until, that is, the wolf visited them again one night and seized an old granny who had been out late to bring in her washing.

A few weeks later, a young mother was eaten on her way back home one night after visiting a friend. And finally, a little child was lost, who had been playing after dark too close to the forest.

The villagers called a meeting. Now it happened that there was a wise old man who lived in a hermit's cave, just outside the village. The people called upon him for help.

'Please rid us of this terrible scourge,' they begged him. They had their own ideas about how this might be done.

'Kill the wolf for us,' some asked him.

'Show us how to surround ourselves with high fences, so that the wolf won't be able to reach us,' others pleaded.

'Turn the wolf into a cuddly lamb that we can tame and pet,' was the request of a third group of villagers.

'I'll see what I can do,' the wise hermit promised, and that very same night, he waited until it was dark, and then he ventured, all alone, into the dense forest. He walked and walked, until he could feel the wolf very close to him. He could hear its breathing and see the green glint of its hungry eyes. For a moment, the wolf and the hermit seemed to be having a deep conversation, then the hermit returned to the village, unharmed.

The next day, the villagers crowded round him. 'Did you kill it?' some of them asked.

'Will you show us how to build our fortress?' others pleaded.

'Have you turned it into a woolly lamb?' demanded the rest.

The hermit shook his head. 'It's much simpler than that,' he told them. 'You only need to feed it!'

At first, the people were aghast. 'How can we feed it?' they asked. 'Why should we feed it,' they complained, 'after all it has done to harm us?' But after a while, at nightfall, when they heard the pad, pad, pad of the wolf prowling through their streets, they would push bowls of food outside – at first, fearfully and resentfully, and then more confidently. Soon, the wolf was a nightly guest. He never again harmed a hair on their heads, and they were proud to be known, throughout the land, as the village that feeds its wolf.

Retelling of a traditional Franciscan story

The Art of
Living True

62

The Fox and the Bear

One day, a man wandered through a forest and came across an injured fox. The poor creature had been pursued by the huntsmen and had broken its legs in its efforts to escape. Now it lay in the undergrowth, helpless to find food.

The man's heart went out to the fox, but as he watched, a grizzly bear loomed up out of the trees, dragging the carcass of an animal it had killed. The bear appeared to ignore the presence of the wounded fox, but when it shuffled off again after its meal, it left the remains of the carcass close to where the fox was hiding. The fox devoured the meat avidly.

The next day, the man walked through the forest again. And again, the bear left a tasty morsel behind for the hungry fox. And on the third day, the same thing happened.

The man pondered hard over what he had seen. 'If God cares so much for a wounded fox,' he thought, 'how much more will he care for me. My faith is far too feeble. I must learn to trust in God as this fox trusts.'

So the man went into a quiet corner of the forest and prayed, 'Loving Father, this injured fox has shown me what it means to trust you. Now I too commit myself entirely to your care. I trust that you will care for me just as you care for the fox.' And with this, he lay down and waited for God to act.

A day passed and nothing happened. The man was getting hungry. A second day passed and still nothing happened. The man was deeply puzzled. A third day passed and the man was angry. 'Father,' he cried, 'you love that little fox more than you love me! Why won't you care for me when I trust you so much? Why don't you feed *me*?'

At last, hunger forced him back into the town. There on the streets the man came upon a starving child. He railed on God in his rage. 'Why don't you *do* something?!'

'I *have* done something,' God said. 'I have created *you*. But you choose to behave like the fox when you could model yourself on the bear.'

Retelling of an Arabian fable

63

The Stranger's Gift

There was once a village that had fallen on very hard times. The villagers had once been very happy, and their community had been famous for its hospitality and friendliness, and the warmth with which it welcomed strangers.

But something had gone wrong in the village. People had begun to bicker with one another. Quarrels broke out for no apparent reason. Rivalry sprang up where once there had been friendship and trust. The chief of the village was very sad about this. He knew that the people would never be happy like this, but he could do nothing to restore the old times of harmony and peace. Strangers no longer wanted to visit the village. The people stopped caring for it. The village was falling into ruin.

But it happened that one day a stranger came by. He approached the village like one with a mission, as though he already knew what he would find there. And very soon, he met the village chief. He recognized the sad expression in his eyes, and the two were soon engaged in a serious conversation.

The village chief told the stranger about his feelings of despair, and his fears that soon the village would disintegrate. The stranger told the village chief that he might know of a way to redeem the lost village and restore it to a real community again.

'Please tell me the secret,' the village chief begged the stranger.

'The secret is very simple,' the stranger said by way of reply. 'The fact is, one of the villagers is actually the Messiah!'

The village chief could hardly believe what he was hearing, yet the stranger had an air of authority about him that was irrefutable.

The stranger left, but the village chief couldn't resist telling his closest friend what the stranger had told him. Soon the rumour ran through the village like wildfire. 'One of us is the Messiah! Can you believe it – somewhere, hidden among our number, the Messiah is living!'

Now, deep down, the villagers were a godly folk who wanted things to be right in their community. The thought that the Messiah himself might be living among them, incognito, made them see things very differently. Could it be the baker? they wondered. Or the postman? Or the old lady who breeds the chickens and sells the eggs? Perhaps it was old Granny Riley, whom the children were in the habit of taunting because of her scarred old face. The speculation went on and on.

But the funny thing was that after the stranger's visit, things were never the same again. People began to treat each other with reverence. They lived like people who had a common purpose, and who were seeking for something very precious together, never quite knowing whether the treasure was actually right in front of them.

Before long, visitors began to come to the village just to be part of the happy, holy atmosphere that prevailed there. The stranger never came back. He didn't need to.

Retelling of a traditional story

64

Rooms to Rent?

God was walking the streets, looking for a home for his son. He knocked on my door. Well, I suppose I could let him rent the little spare bedroom, I thought. He read my thoughts. 'I was looking to buy,' he said.

'Oh, I don't think I really want to sell,' I replied. 'I need the place for myself, you see. But you could use the back room. The rent's quite low. Why don't you come in and have a look?'

So he came in, and he looked around. 'I like it,' he said. 'I'll take it on your own terms.'

Once he was settled in, I began to wonder whether I'd been a bit mean. There he was, cooped up in that little spare bedroom. God must have been having similar thoughts, because he was there again at my door.

'Would you have any more space now, do you think?' he asked gently.

'Well, I've been thinking, and I could offer your son an extra room to rent now.'

'Thank you,' said God. 'I'll take the extra room. Maybe you'll decide to give my son more room later on. Meanwhile, I like what I see.'

Time went on. I was still feeling a bit uneasy about this transaction. 'I'd like to give you some more room,' I kept telling God, 'but you see, it's a bit difficult. I need some space for *me*.'

'I understand,' God kept saying. 'I'll wait. I like what I see.'

Eventually, I decided to offer God the whole of the top floor. He accepted gratefully, on behalf of his son. 'Well, I can spare it really,' I told him. 'I'd really like to let you have the whole house, but I'm not sure…'

'I understand,' said God. 'I'll wait. I like what I see.'

A bit more time went by, and there was God again at my door. 'I just want you to know', he said, 'that I'm still very interested in buying your house. I wouldn't put you out. We'd work it out together. Your house would be mine and my son would live here.'

'Actually,' he added, 'you'd have more space than ever before.'

'I really can't see how that could be true,' I replied, hesitating on the doorstep.

'I know,' said God. 'And to be honest, I can't really explain it. It's something you have to discover for yourself. It only happens if you let my son have the whole house.'

'A bit risky,' I said.

'Yes, but try me,' encouraged God.

'I'm not sure. I'll let you know.'

'I'll wait,' said God. 'I like what I see.'

Source unknown

65

A Sandwich for Supper

A story tells of a man who went to the office every day in his expensive car, and made important decisions and signed big contracts. Often, the important man would enjoy business lunches with his clients, and would try to distract the attention of his influential guests away from the unsavoury spectacle of the beggars on the streets of his city.

One evening, after a hard day making money, he packed his briefcase to go home, where supper would be waiting for him. As he was locking his desk for the night, he caught sight of a stale sandwich lying abandoned at the back of the drawer. Without much thought he crammed it in his coat pocket. No need for it to go mouldy and mess up his desk. And on the way out to the car park he saw a street beggar on the steps, huddled in an old blanket. 'Here, my friend,' he said to the beggar. 'Here is something for your supper.' And he gave him the stale sandwich.

That night, the man dreamed that he was away on a business trip. After the day's meeting, he was taken with his fellow directors to the town's most luxurious restaurant. Everyone gave their orders and settled down with their aperitifs to look forward to a convivial evening.

The orders arrived. Pâté de foie gras. Medallions of venison. Lamb cutlets with rosemary and garlic. The dishes being brought to the table brought gasps of delight from all the company. Then his own order appeared. A waitress set in front of him one small plate, on which was served a stale sandwich.

'What kind of service is this?' the man demanded, enraged. 'This isn't what I ordered! I thought this was the best restaurant in town!'

'Oh sir,' the waitress told him, 'you've been misinformed. This isn't a restaurant at all. This is heaven. We are only able to serve you what you sent on ahead while you were alive. I'm very sorry, sir, but when we looked under your name, the best we could find to serve to you was this little sandwich.'

Retelling of a Jewish folk story

66

A Teaspoon of Oil

A certain shopkeeper sent his son to learn about the secret of happiness from the wisest man in the world. The lad wandered through the desert for forty days, and finally came upon a beautiful castle, high atop a mountain. It was there that the wise man lived.

Rather than finding a saintly man, though, our hero, on entering the main room of the castle, saw a hive of activity: tradesmen came and went, people were conversing in the corners, a small orchestra was playing soft music, and there was a table covered with platters of the most delicious food in that part of the world. The wise man conversed with everyone, and the boy had to wait for two hours before it was his turn to be given the man's attention.

The wise man listened attentively to the boy's explanation of why he had come, but told him that he didn't have time just then to explain the secret of happiness. He suggested that the boy look around the palace and return in two hours.

'Meanwhile, I want to ask you to do something,' said the wise man, handing the boy a teaspoon that held two drops of oil. 'As you wander around, carry this spoon with you without allowing the oil to spill.'

The boy began climbing and descending the many stairways of the palace, keeping his eyes fixed on the spoon. After two hours he returned to the room where the wise man was.

'Well,' asked the wise man, 'did you see the Persian tapestries that are hanging in my dining hall? Did you see the garden that it took the master gardener ten years to create? Did you notice the beautiful parchments in my library?'

The boy was embarrassed, and confessed that he had observed nothing. His only concern had been not to spill the oil that the wise man had entrusted to him.

'Then go back and observe the marvels of my world,' said the wise man. 'You cannot trust a man if you don't know his house.'

Relieved, the boy picked up the spoon and returned to his exploration of the palace, this time observing all of the works of art on the ceilings and the walls. He saw the gardens, the mountains all around him, the beauty of the flowers and the taste with which everything had been selected. Upon returning to the wise man, he related in detail everything he had seen.

'But where are the drops of oil I entrusted to you?' asked the wise man.

Looking down at the spoon he held, the boy saw that the oil was gone.

'Well, there is only one piece of advice I can give you,' said the wisest of wise men. 'The secret of happiness is to see all the marvels of the world, and never to forget the drops of oil on the spoon.'

Paulo Coelho

The Three Sieves

Janice came rushing into her grandma's house. 'Gran, Gran, there's something I'm dying to tell you…'

'Wait a moment,' her grandma broke in with a wise smile. 'Whatever it is you want to tell me, have you shaken it through the three sieves?'

'Three sieves?' Janice asked, puzzled.

'Yes, my love. Three sieves! Let's see whether your story will go through the three sieves. The first sieve is the truth. Have you thought about whether what you are going to tell me is true?'

'Well,' hesitated Janice. 'I heard it from someone else, so I'm not absolutely sure…'

'Right,' said Gran. 'That was an honest answer. So let's try it through the second sieve. This is the sieve of goodness. Since what you are going to tell me is not necessarily true, then is it at least something good?'

Janice lowered her eyes. 'Well no,' she admitted. 'Not really. In fact, quite the opposite.'

'Well,' the wise grandma continued, 'let's use the third sieve, and see whether what you are going to tell me, even if neither true nor good, is at least necessary.'

'Well, not exactly necessary…' Janice sank into a thoughtful silence.

'So,' Gran said, giving Janice an understanding hug, 'since what you were going to tell me is neither true, nor good, nor necessary, I suggest that we bury it deep in the ground of forgetfulness, where it won't cause any heartache to anyone ever again.'

Source unknown

Two Brothers

Two brothers once worked together to run the family farm. They were loving brothers, each one always looking out for the well-being of the other. They shared all the farm produce equally, and they also shared the work fairly.

However, one of the brothers was a single man, and the other was married with a family. The single brother thought about this fact, and he came to the conclusion that their habit of equal sharing was, after all, unjust. 'I am just one,' he thought to himself, 'but my brother has to feed not just himself, but his wife and children too.' So with this thought in mind, he decided that his brother should have a larger share of the produce than he did, and in the middle of the night, he got up and quietly took a sack of grain from his own store and placed it in his brother's. This became a habit, and he regularly took extra produce across to his brother's store. And so the years passed.

Meanwhile, the married brother was also thinking things through. 'I am married,' he thought to himself. 'I have a wife who cares for me, and strong children who help me with the farm work. My brother has no one to support him. It isn't fair that I should take as much as he does from the produce of the farm.' So he too began to get up in the night, and to take some of his own share of the produce over to his brother's store.

This went on for several years, and neither brother could understand why his own stock of produce never seemed to diminish, even though each was giving some of it away regularly to his brother.

Then it happened that one dark night, they both set off to visit their brother's store at exactly the same moment; and so, each carrying his sack, they met each other in the middle of the field between their two cottages. At first, they were both shocked by this unplanned encounter, but they soon realized what they were doing. They dropped their sacks of grain and embraced each other.

Source unknown

The Muddy Road

Tanzan and Ekido were once travelling together down a muddy road. A heavy rain was still falling.

Coming around a bend, they met a lovely girl in a silk kimono and sash, unable to cross the intersection.

'Come on, girl,' said Tanzan at once. Lifting her in his arms, he carried her over the mud.

Ekido did not speak again until that night when they reached a lodging temple. Then he no longer could restrain himself. 'We monks don't go near females,' he told Tanzan, 'especially not young and lovely ones. It is dangerous. Why did you do that?'

'I left the girl there,' said Tanzan. 'Are you still carrying her?'

Source unknown

Two Questions

There was once a king who was overburdened with the tasks of state. One day, he commented to his wife, 'If only I could know which matters were the most important, I could use my time more effectively and be a better king.'

So the queen urged him to consult with the wise men of the kingdom. One by one the king called the wise men to him: scholars and priests, politicians and counsellors. Each had a different view about which matters were the most important.

Eventually, almost despairing of getting helpful advice, the king set off to visit a holy hermit who lived in the hills. As he approached the hermit's dwelling, he saw the holy man digging his garden. The hermit hardly interrupted his work as he listened attentively to the king's request for advice. 'I have two questions,' explained the king. 'On whom should I spend my time and focus my attention?' and, 'Which affairs are the most important, and should therefore be taken care of first?'

The hermit listened in silence and continued to dig his garden.

The king realized that the hermit was struggling and tired. 'Here,' he said, 'I see you are tired. Give me the spade and I will do some digging for you.' The hermit thanked him and handed him the spade.

The king dug the hermit's garden for two hours, before asking him the two questions again, but still the hermit did not answer. Instead, he took back the spade with the comment, 'You rest now, and I'll dig.'

But the king refused, and he went on digging until sundown. When he finally put down the spade, he said to the hermit, 'I came to ask you two questions. Since you cannot, or will not, answer me, I will go home now.'

The hermit replied, 'See, someone is running here. Let's see who it is.'

The king turned to see a bearded man running towards them, clutching his hands to a wound in his stomach. As he reached the king, he fell to the ground, moaning.

The hermit and the king quickly washed and dressed the man's wound as best they could, and the king bound the wound up with one of his own handkerchiefs and one of the hermit's clean rags. After a while, the blood stopped flowing from the wound, and the man asked for a drink of water. The hermit gave him a drink, and together the hermit and the king carried the man into the hermit's hut and laid him on the bed. Exhausted after the day's work, the king also fell asleep.

The next morning, when he awoke, the king saw that the wounded man was staring at him. 'Forgive me,' he begged the king.

'I don't know you,' the king replied. 'I have no reason to need to forgive you.'

Then the man confessed, 'I had sworn vengeance on you for executing my brother, and I followed you here to the hermit's home, planning to kill you. When you didn't return for so long, I came out of my hiding place, and was caught by your bodyguards, who recognized me and attacked me. I managed to escape, but I would have bled to death if you had not taken care of me. I wanted to kill you, but you saved my life. From now on, I will be your most faithful servant. Forgive me.'

Quickly, the king forgave the man and promised to have him cared for until his full health was restored.

Leaving the man, the king returned to the hermit, who was digging his garden again, just as on the previous day. 'For the last time,' he pleaded, 'will you answer my two questions? Otherwise I shall go away.'

'But you have had your answers,' the hermit replied.

'I don't understand,' retorted the king.

'Yesterday,' the hermit explained, 'you had compassion for my weariness, and you stayed here to help me dig my garden. If you had gone straight home, our friend here would have attacked you. So the most important task was to show compassion. Later, when the man appeared here, it was the time to care for him and bind his wounds. Had you not done so, he would have died and would never have been able to make his peace with you. At that moment, he was the most important person, and caring for him was your most important task.

'So the answer to your questions is this: there is only ever one important time, and that is "now". And the most important person is the one who stands before us now. God gives us one opportunity at a time. The person I am with now and the task that lies immediately ahead of me are always more important than either the past or the future. The past has gone. The future may never happen. The present is the only reality.'

Retelling of a story by Leo Tolstoy

The Obedient and the Disobedient Servants

A king had two servants. He told the first servant to do something. The servant did it, and was promoted. He told the second servant to do something. The servant did not do it, and was fired.

The servant who was promoted lived very, very well in the king's service, and continued to obey the king and be promoted. One day, however, his thoughts turned to the servant who had disobeyed the king and been fired. So he went to visit him.

He arrived at the house where the man used to live, but he was no longer there. A neighbour said he had sold the house and moved to a much smaller one.

When the first servant arrived at the place where the second servant now lived, he realized that 'house' was too kind a word. It was a hovel. The first servant knocked on the door, and a voice said, 'Come in!'

The second servant was sitting on the dirt floor eating a very, very thin soup.

The servant who had been promoted smiled. 'If you had learned to obey the king, you would not have to eat that thin soup,' he said.

The servant who had been fired said, 'If you had learned how to eat this soup, you would not have to obey the king!'

John Shea

Patience and Determination

The Power of the Flame

Once upon a time, there was a piece of iron that was very strong. One after another, the axe, the saw, the hammer and the flame tried to break it.

'I'll master it,' said the axe. Its blows fell heavily on the iron, but every blow made its edge more blunt, until it ceased to strike.

'Leave it to me,' said the saw, and it worked backwards and forwards on the iron's surface until its jagged teeth were all worn and broken. Then it fell aside.

'Ah!' said the hammer. 'I knew you wouldn't succeed. I'll show you the way.' But at the first blow, off flew its head and the iron remained as before.

'Shall I try?' asked the small, soft flame.

'Forget it,' all replied. 'What can you do?'

But the flame curled around the iron, embraced it and never left it until the iron melted under the flame's irresistible influence.

Aesop

73

The Frog Who Wouldn't Give Up

Once upon a time, there were two frogs. One morning, they were jumping up and down on the shiny, scrubbed floor of the dairy in a farmhouse.

The farmer's wife caught sight of these two frogs, and she took hold of a big broomstick to chase them out of the dairy. 'I won't have dirty amphibians jumping up and down on my shiny dairy floor,' she scolded.

In their panic, the frogs looked for somewhere to hide away, out of the range of the fearsome broom and the angry farmer's wife.

'Quick, over here,' said one frog to the other. 'I can see a hiding place where the broom will never reach us.'

So they hopped into a corner of the dairy, as fast as their little froggy legs would carry them.

'Now jump, as high as you know how,' said the first frog to the second.

So they jumped. High, and higher, and highest. They jumped higher than they had ever managed to jump before. They jumped right over the big, grey wall of the hiding place.

'Plop!' they landed, only to find themselves in a bucket of fresh cream, newly drawn off the milking pail.

'Oh dear,' said the second frog to the first. 'That's it! We're done for! No chance of getting out of here.'

'Keep paddling,' said the first frog. 'There must be a way out. We'll think of something.'

'But I'm so tired after all that jumping up and down on the dairy floor,' complained the second frog. 'And I've completely exhausted myself making that great leap which landed me in this bucket. I haven't got any energy left to paddle around in a bucket of cream. It's no use,' he croaked. 'It's too thick to swim in, too thin to walk on and too slippery to crawl out of. We've had it. We're not going to get out of here alive.'

And with that, he gave up, sank down to the bottom of the bucket and died.

But his friend kept on paddling. He paddled all through the long, lonely, weary night. He often felt like giving up and joining his friend at the bottom of the bucket. But something made him keep on paddling.

Eventually, the sun rose again, and the first beams of light came streaking across the dairy.

The frog who wouldn't give up looked down at the cream, tears of exhaustion welling up in his little froggy eyes.

And to his amazement, he discovered that he was standing on a mountain of butter, which he had churned all by himself.

Source unknown

Good Luck... Bad Luck?

There was once an old man who had one son and a horse. One day, his horse broke free and went galloping off to freedom in the nearby hills.

The man's neighbours sympathized with him. 'What very bad luck to have lost your horse,' they said.

'Why do you say that?' replied the old man. 'Who is to say whether it is bad luck?'

And sure enough, the very next night the horse returned, and behind him came twelve wild horses, which he had led back home with him. The man's son quickly closed the gate of the paddock, and instead of one horse, they now had thirteen.

And the neighbours stared at the paddock the next morning and said, 'What extraordinary good luck – to have thirteen horses!'

'Why do you say that?' the old man replied. 'Who is to say whether it is good luck?'

A little while later, the old man's son went out riding one of the new horses. But the horse was still wild, and it threw the boy off its back, and the boy fell and broke his leg.

The neighbours came round to the old man to commiserate. 'What very bad luck', they said, 'that your son has broken his leg.'

'Why do you say that?' the old man asked them. 'Who is to say whether it is bad luck?'

And indeed, a short while later, the militia came to the village, conscripting all the able-bodied young men to go to fight in the war, where many of them would lose their lives. But when they saw the old man's son lying there with a broken leg, they passed him by and went on their way.

'How lucky you are,' the neighbours said. And the old man smiled.

Source unknown

The Hidden Emerald

The old man leafed through the book, and fell to reading a page he came to. The boy waited, and then interrupted the old man, just as he himself had been interrupted.

'Why are you telling me all this?'

'Because you are trying to realize your destiny. And you are at the point where you're about to give it all up.'

'And that's where you always appear on the scene?'

'Not always in this way, but I always appear in one form or another. Sometimes I appear in the form of a solution, or a good idea. At other times, at a crucial moment, I make it easier for things to happen. There are other things I do, too, but most of the time people don't realize I've done them.'

The old man related that, the week before, he had been forced to appear before a miner, and had taken the form of a stone.

The miner had abandoned everything to go mining for emeralds. For five years he had been working a certain river, and had examined hundreds of thousands of stones looking for an emerald. The miner was about to give it all up, right at the point when, if he were to examine just one more stone – just *one* more – he would find his emerald.

Since the miner had sacrificed everything to his destiny, the old man decided to become involved. He transformed himself into a stone, which rolled up to the miner's foot. The miner, with all the anger and frustration of his five fruitless years, picked up the stone and threw it aside. But he had thrown it with such force that it broke the stone it fell on, and there, embedded in the broken stone, was the most beautiful emerald in the world.

Paulo Coelho

A Letter with a Difference

There was once a mother who had two daughters. She loved her daughters dearly, but from their earliest years, the two girls would quarrel and fight with each other. As they grew older, their enmity hardened, and they became totally estranged from each other. As adults, they would have no contact with each other. They grew completely apart.

As you can imagine, this caused the mother great pain. She agonized about how she might possibly bring them back together again. And then she had an idea. She got out her pen, and she wrote a letter to them both. In this letter, she told them, over and over again, how very much she loved them both, and how she longed for them to love each other in the way that she loved each of them. She told them how much it grieved her that they were separated. And she gave them news of herself, and some guidance on how they might live happier and more loving lives themselves.

When the letter was ready, she wrote out one copy for each daughter, but these copies were special. Each copy contained only every second sentence of the original letter. So the copy for one daughter had only the even sentences, and the other daughter's copy contained only the odd sentences. Neither copy made sense on its own. Neither contained the fullness of the mother's message.

When the two daughters received their letters, they were puzzled, until it dawned on them what had happened. Then they faced a dilemma. If they really wanted to know what their loving mother had written, they would have to put their two letters together and read them as one. And that meant that they would have to approach one another again in mutual love and respect.

For a long time, the mother waited in vain for an answer to her letter. There were questions, from both the daughters. There were complicated efforts on both their parts to make sense of the half-letter each of them possessed. There were recriminations. Each daughter thought she knew her mother better than her sister ever could. Each daughter believed that her mother loved her more than she could possibly love her other daughter.

Then one day, when the mother had almost given up hope, there was a knock at the door. There they stood, together. 'We've come home,' they said in unison. 'We've finally put our letters together, and we've come to say how much we love you, Mum.' And she flung her arms round them both, tears of joy streaming across her cheeks, and welcomed them back home.

Retelling of a traditional story

77

Only the Seed

Once upon a time, a pilgrim set out on the long journey in search of peace, joy and love. The pilgrim walked for many weary miles, and time passed.

Gradually, the young, lively steps became slower and more laboured. The pilgrim's journey passed through landscapes that were not always happy ones. Through war. Through sickness. Through quarrels and rejections and separations. A land where, it seemed, the more people possessed, the more warlike they became – the more they had to defend, the more they needed to attack each other. Longing for peace, they prepared for war. Longing for love, they surrounded themselves with walls of distrust and barriers of fear. Longing for life, they were walking deeper into death.

But one morning, the pilgrim came to a little cottage at the wayside. Something about this little cottage attracted the pilgrim. It was as though it was lit up from the inside. Full of curiosity, the pilgrim went inside. And inside the cottage was a little shop, and behind the counter stood a shopkeeper. It was hard to judge the age – hard even to say for sure whether it was a man or a woman. There was an air of timelessness about the place.

'What would you like?' asked the shopkeeper in a kindly voice.

'What do you stock here?' asked the pilgrim.

'Oh, we have all the things here that you most long for,' replied the shopkeeper. 'Just tell me what you desire.' The pilgrim hardly knew where to begin. So many desires came rushing to mind at once.

'I want peace – in my own family, in my native land and in the whole world.

'I want to make something good of my life.

'I want those who are sick to be well again and those who are lonely to have friends.

'I want those who are hungry to have enough to eat.

'I want every child born on this planet today to have a chance to be educated.

'I want everyone on earth to live in freedom.

'I want this world to be a kingdom of love.'

There was a pause while the pilgrim reviewed this shopping list.

Gently, the shopkeeper broke in. 'I'm sorry,' came the quiet reply. 'I should have explained. We don't supply the fruits here. We only supply the seeds.'

Source unknown

78

The Touchstone

It is said that when the Great Library of Alexandria was burned down, only one book survived. It was a very ordinary book, dull and uninteresting, so it was sold for a few pennies to a poor man who barely knew how to read.

Now that book, dull and uninteresting as it seemed, was probably the most valuable book in the world, for on the inside of the back cover were scrawled, in large round letters, a few sentences that contained the secret of the Touchstone – a tiny pebble that could turn anything it touched into pure gold.

The writing declared that this precious pebble was lying somewhere on the shore of the Black Sea, among thousands of other pebbles that were exactly like it, except in one particular – that whereas all the other pebbles were cold to the touch, this one was warm, as if it were alive. The man rejoiced in his good luck. He sold everything he had, borrowed a large sum of money, which would last him a year, and made for the Black Sea, where he set up his tent and began a painstaking search for the Touchstone.

This was the way he went about it. He would lift a pebble. If it was cold to the touch, he would not throw it back on the shore because if he did that, he might be lifting and feeling the same stone dozens of times. No, he would throw it into the sea. So each day, for hours on end, he persevered in his patient endeavour: lift a pebble; if it felt cold, throw it into the sea; lift another… and so on, endlessly.

He spent a week, a month, ten months, a whole year at this task. Then he borrowed some more money and kept at it for another two years. On and on he went: lift a pebble; hold it; feel that it was cold; throw it back into the sea. Hour after hour; day after day; week after week… still no Touchstone.

One evening, he picked up a pebble and it was warm to the touch – but through sheer force of habit, he threw it into the Black Sea!

Anthony de Mello

Confrontation

The country was at war. The people were terrified, and had fled to the hills in the face of the advancing enemy troops. By the time the army arrived, the place was deserted. The fierce-looking barbarian of a general called his troops together. 'Where has everyone gone?' he demanded, raging.

'They have all fled in fear of us,' the men replied.

'Is there no one left to pay tribute? No citizens that we can force into slavery? No one to terrorize, and no treasure to plunder?' The general's rage knew no bounds.

'As far as we can discover, the only person here for miles around is an old holy man living in a hermitage just outside the village.'

Without any more ado, the general marched to the hermitage and demanded to see the holy man. After a search, he found him quietly meditating.

The general was furious that the holy man refused to acknowledge him as conqueror. He shouted at the holy man: 'Don't you know who I am? You are looking at the man who could strike you dead without batting an eyelid!'

The holy man raised his eyes and fixed his gaze steadily on the raging commander.

'Don't you know,' he asked calmly, 'that you are looking at a man who can be struck dead without batting an eyelid?'

For a moment the general was speechless, fixed by the cool gaze of the holy man. Then he bowed low, called his troops together, and left the village without doing any further damage.

Retelling of a traditional oriental story

The Basket of Dreams

There was once a herdsman who lived alone on the plains. His only company was his cattle. He loved those cattle. Every morning, he would rise before dawn to milk them. Then he would take them to a place where they could graze. At dusk he would bring them inside the thorny fence of his kraal to keep them safe from the leopards and hyenas prowling in the night.

One morning, when the herdsman went to milk his cows, he found their udders wrinkled and empty of milk. Strange. That had never happened before. So he took them to the best grazing he knew, a stretch of lush, long grass beside a stream.

But next morning, the cows' udders were still dry. Very strange. Again he took the cattle to good pasture. But he was suspicious now. That night he did not go to bed. When he had brought the cattle inside the kraal, he hid behind the door flap of his house and kept watch.

Clouds were drifting across the moon. Presently, a gap opened in the clouds and a shaft of moonlight shone upon the sleeping cattle. Three women came walking down the moonbeam, their hips swaying, their skin shining, and each one carried on her head a giant calabash. The herdsman was amazed by their beauty.

When the women reached the ground, they began to collect the milk from the cows in their calabashes. Suddenly the herdsman came to his senses. These women were stealing his milk! He leapt out and chased the women round and round the cattle. Two of the women were too quick for him. They hoisted their calabashes, nearly filled, onto their heads and fled away up the moonbeam. But the third woman was too slow. The herdsman grabbed her before she could escape. She struggled, but could not break free.

Then the gap in the clouds closed and the moonbeam was gone. The woman stopped struggling. The herdsman let go of her. They looked at each other and neither of them knew what to do. So the herdsman said, 'Since you've milked the cattle, you may as well come in for a cup of tea.'

As they drank the tea, the herdsman watched the woman's face in the firelight. She looked so beautiful. He began to realize just how lonely he had been. He didn't want this woman to go away. So he asked her to stay and be his wife.

She said, 'I would gladly be your wife. But first I must return to the place I have come from, because I have some things that I need to bring.'

'But if you return there,' said the herdsman, 'how can I be sure that you will come back to me?'

'You cannot be sure that I will,' said the woman, 'but I will.'

So saying, she went away. All night and all the next day, the herdsman waited. And the following night another moonbeam shone into the kraal and the woman returned. Under her arm she carried a tightly woven basket with a close-fitting lid.

She told the herdsman, 'I will be your wife, but you must promise never to look inside this basket.'

The herdsman promised and the two of them lived together happily. Each day, while he watched the cattle on the plain, she would gather nuts, roots and herbs in the forest.

By the fire after dark, the woman would sometimes take the lid off her basket and look inside. When she gazed into the basket, the herdsman would see on her face a look of such delight and longing that he had never seen when she looked at him. He began to feel jealous. He wondered what was in that basket, and whether it might have something to do with someone else.

Some evenings, the woman got home later than he did. While he waited for her, he would stare at the basket in the corner. He began to say to himself, 'Now that we are husband and wife, everything that we have belongs to us both. All that is mine is hers. All that is hers is mine. So if I were to look inside that basket, I'd simply be looking at something that is mine anyway.'

One moonlit night, when his wife was especially late coming home, the herdsman could restrain himself no longer. He pulled off the basket's lid and looked inside. And saw that the basket was empty. He laughed a scornful laugh, but his laughter soon changed to anger as he realized that the woman had been testing him. He was so angry that he threw the basket and lid on the floor. So when the woman came in, these were the first things she saw.

'You looked,' she said.

'Yes, I looked!' the herdsman shouted. 'Why have you been playing this game with me? Telling me I mustn't look in the basket – when there's nothing *in* the basket!'

'You saw nothing?'

'It's empty!'

'Oh no,' said the woman. 'It's not empty. That basket contains everything that is most important to me. All my hopes. All my dreams. If only you had waited, I would have shown you everything.'

Sadly she picked up the basket and went outside. A shaft of moonlight was shining on the sleeping cattle. As the herdsman watched from the doorway, the woman climbed slowly up the moonbeam. She got smaller and smaller. Then the gap in the clouds closed and the woman vanished with the moonbeam. And that was the last time the herdsman ever saw her.

A retelling by Anthony Nanson

81

Bamboo

Once upon a time, in the heart of an ancient kingdom, there was a garden. The master of the kingdom would often walk through the garden in the cool of the evening, and there he would visit his favourite tree, the lovely and gracious Bamboo.

Year by year, Bamboo grew lovelier and more gracious. She loved the master, and her greatest desire was to dance for him. When the breeze blew through her branches, she would sway backwards and forwards, tossing and bowing, and dancing her very best, just for the master's eyes. And the master's heart leapt with joy to see his beloved Bamboo.

One day, the master came to visit Bamboo. His brow was furrowed, and he was in deep thought.

Bamboo saw him approaching, and she danced for him, full of passion and adoration, her fronds sweeping the ground before him in a loving greeting.

'My Bamboo,' said the master. 'You know how I love you. Today, I would ask you to help me in an important task.'

Bamboo was thrilled. There was nothing she would not do at her master's request. 'Tell me, master,' she replied. 'What can I do for you? I am ready. Tell me what I can do. Use me as you will.'

The master's eyes were troubled as he spoke the words: 'My beloved Bamboo. I need you, and I must cut you down in order to use you for my great task.'

Bamboo shook with horror. 'Cut me down?' she cried. 'But master, how shall I dance for you? How shall I show my love for you? Shall I never dance for you ever again?'

But the master was firm. 'My dear Bamboo, if I do not cut you down, I cannot use you.'

Despair froze the heart of poor Bamboo as she consented. 'Then do what you must do, master,' she said quietly.

And so the master cut down Bamboo. She lay trembling at his feet, with only her fronds and leaves to shelter her from the cold air.

And again, the master bent over her, and gazed at her with compassion.

'If I am to use you, dear Bamboo, I must cut off your leaves and fronds.'

A sick cold seeped into Bamboo's heart. She gave her grieved consent as the master cut off her fronds and leaves and left her naked and shorn on the bare earth of the garden.

But the worst was still to come. Again, the master spoke gently to his beloved: 'If I am to use you, I must now split you in two and cut out your centre. I must scoop out the heart of you.'

'Oh master,' cried Bamboo. 'Must this really be? Would you do this to me?'

'I cannot use you, dear Bamboo, unless you consent to be split and emptied.'

'Then,' consented Bamboo, 'do what you must do. Split me and cut me and hollow out my centre.'

So the master split Bamboo, and hollowed her out, and gently lifted her to a place in the garden where a fresh, sparkling spring flowed. There he laid her down, placing one end of her in the sparkling spring, and the other in the dry field beyond the garden. The water sang to Bamboo as it leapt along the channel of her broken, empty heart. The water flooded the dried field, and the master planted a new crop. The days passed. Fresh green shoots appeared. Soon it was harvest time.

At harvest time, Bamboo, once so gracious as she danced to the master of the garden, was even more gracious in her brokenness, bringing new life to the whole field. Once she had been life abundant; now she was the bringer of abundant life to the world beyond the garden.

Retelling of a traditional story

82

The Sunflower (सूरजमुखी) and the Sparrow

Between an old wooden chest and a rusty washing-machine drum a little sunflower grew. She was surrounded by rubbish and dereliction. She was the only flower for miles around. Why the sunflower should be growing there, of all places, no one knew.

The flower was often sad, and at night, she would dream of lush meadows, of fields of bright flowers where the butterflies flew around her.

One day a bedraggled little sparrow came and perched in front of her and gazed at her, his beak hanging open.

'How beautiful you are,' he chirped. 'Really beautiful.'

'I'm not,' retorted the sunflower sadly. 'You should see my sisters. They're ten times my size. I'm small and ugly.'

'For me, you're the most beautiful of them all,' piped the sparrow, and flew away.

The bird visited the sunflower every day from then on. And every day, the sunflower grew a little taller, and every day, her flower became a little brighter. They became friends.

But one day the sparrow didn't come. And the next day he didn't come. And the next. The sunflower was very worried. Then one morning, when she awoke, she saw the sparrow lying in front of her, his wings outstretched. What a shock it gave her. 'Are you dead, my little friend? What's happened?'

Slowly, the bird opened his eyes. 'For the last few days, I've not found anything to eat on the waste tip. Now I haven't got any strength left. I've come to you so that I can die close to you.'

'No. No!' cried the sunflower. 'Wait. Wait just a moment!' She lowered her heavy flower-head towards him, and a few sunflower seeds fell to the ground. 'Pick them up, my little friend. They will give you new strength.' The sparrow cracked open a few of the seeds with his last ounce of energy, and lay still, exhausted.

But the next day, he was already feeling stronger. He wanted to thank the sunflower, but he was devastated when he saw her. Her yellow flower petals had all gone limp, and her leaves hung down lifelessly. 'What's the matter with you, sunflower?' he chirped in his distress.

'Don't be concerned for me,' said the sunflower weakly. 'My time is over. Do you know what? I always thought that my existence was meaningless, here on the waste tip. But now I know that there is a purpose for everything, even though we can't always understand it. Without you, I would have lost my will to live, and without me, you would have lost your life. And look, there are still plenty of sunflower seeds on the ground. Leave a few of them behind, and maybe one day there will be lots of sunflowers here, and lots of bedraggled sparrows will fly around them, like butterflies.'

Retelling of a traditional German story

Sacrifice

The Beggar-King

There was once a king who had no son and longed for an heir who would succeed him to the throne. So he posted a notice, inviting young men to apply to be considered for adoption into his family, to become his heir. All that he asked of the applicants was that they should love God and love their neighbour.

A poor peasant boy saw the notice, but he thought that he would have no chance of being adopted by the king because of the ragged clothes he wore. So he worked very hard, until he had just enough money to buy a new set of clothes. Wearing his new clothes, he then set off to the royal palace to apply for the position of the king's adopted son.

Now, as he was journeying towards the palace, the boy met a poor beggar on the road. The old man was shivering with cold, and the boy felt sorry for him and exchanged clothes with him.

As he was now back to wearing beggar's clothes, it hardly seemed worth going on towards the king's palace. However, having come so far already, the boy decided to keep going and at least see the king's palace from the outside.

When he arrived, he was greeted by scornful laughter and sneering remarks from the king's courtiers. Nevertheless, he was finally admitted into the presence of the king.

There was something strangely familiar about the king. At first, the boy couldn't work out what it was, and why he felt so at home in his presence. Then he realized that the king himself was wearing the clothes that he had given to the old beggar just a few hours ago along the road.

The king came down from his throne and embraced the boy, holding him close in his arms.

'Welcome, my son,' he said.

Source unknown

She-Who-Sits-Alone

A terrible time once befell the Comanche people. It was a time of drought. The land was dying and the people were dying too. In their despair, they called upon the Great Spirit.

'Great Spirit,' they implored, 'our land is dying and our people are dying. How have we angered you? Bring an end to this drought and save your people, for soon there will be nothing left alive.'

And so they prayed, and they danced. They waited, and they prayed. But no rain came. And the little ones and the old ones suffered, and no one knew how to end the suffering.

But there was one small girl who had not yet died of hunger. Her name was She-Who-Sits-Alone. Sitting alone, she watched her people pray and dance, and she held her beloved doll in her arms. The doll was her intimate companion, her second self, dressed in its warrior clothing, with a bone belt and beaded leggings, and bearing the feathers of the blue jay on its head.

She-Who-Sits-Alone watched, with her doll, as the elders went up to the top of the mountain to receive the wisdom of the Great Spirit. Several times did the sun rise above the mountain, and several times did the light fade behind the mountain's bulk before they returned.

On the mountain top, the people gathered round to hear the message of the Great Spirit, and this is what the Great Spirit said to them: 'For many generations, the people have taken from the earth whatever they needed and wanted, but they have given nothing back to the earth. Now the earth is in distress, and the people must make a sacrifice. They must bring to the fire of sacrifice their most treasured possessions. The ashes of the sacrifice must be scattered to the four winds. When this has been done, the rains will come and the earth will live again.'

The people gave thanks and then returned to their tepees to search out their most treasured possessions.

'Surely the Great Spirit does not want my bow,' said the archer.

'Nor could the Great Spirit possibly desire my treasured blanket,' said the mother.

'I know that the Great Spirit could not be asking for my herbs,' said the medicine man.

And so it continued. Everyone had a reason not to give the Great Spirit their greatest treasure.

Meanwhile, She-Who-Sits-Alone took her warrior doll into her arms, held it tight and whispered, 'It is you the Great Spirit desires. I know what I must do.'

So that night, when everyone slept, She-Who-Sits-Alone threw off her sleeping blanket and climbed to the top of the mountain, carrying her warrior doll in one hand and a lighted stick from the campfire in the other. When she reached the mountain top, she spoke to the Great Spirit.

'Great Spirit,' she said, 'here is my warrior doll, the gift of my mother and my father before they died, and my most treasured possession. Please accept it.' As she kindled the fire, she wept, and she remembered her parents and grandparents and friends who had died of hunger, and she thrust her doll into the flames.

Soon the fire died down. She gathered the cooling ashes and cast them to the four winds. Exhausted, she lay down on the mountain top and fell asleep.

When the rising sun kissed her awake the next morning, she looked around, dazed. There, where she had offered her sacrifice, lay a shining feather of the blue jay. And as she knelt to look more closely, the first drops of rain caressed her face.

From then on, She-Who-Sits-Alone was given a new name by her grateful people. She became known as One-Who-Loved-Her-People.

Retelling of a Comanche legend

85

The Christmas Gift

Julia counted out the contents of her purse: just a few pounds. That was all she had, and it was Christmas Eve. How could she possibly buy a Christmas gift for her young husband, Jim, with so little money?

She curled up on the sofa and wept. Then, pulling herself together, she stood up, smoothed her hair back, freshened up her tear-stained face, and had an idea.

There were two possessions in the house that they especially treasured. One was Jim's gold watch. The other was her beautiful, long, wavy hair.

'I know what I'll do!' she exclaimed. 'I'll sell my hair. Then I will have the money to buy him a Christmas gift.'

No sooner said than done, she found a shop that would buy her hair. Soon she had fifty pounds in her pocket – the price of her lovely locks. She made her way to a jeweller's shop, and spent the money on a fine watch strap. 'At last,' she thought to herself, 'he will be able to wear his watch proudly, on this fine strap.' Until that time, Jim hadn't been able to wear his watch, because it had such a shabby worn-out strap.

By now, it was late afternoon. Jim arrived home. When he saw his wife's short hair he turned pale. She flung her arms around his neck. 'Don't worry,' she assured him. 'It will grow again. And I like it like this, anyway.'

For a moment, she thought he was going to cry. Her heart sank as he handed her a little box. 'Happy Christmas, my love,' he said. 'But I'm afraid this gift will be useless.'

She opened the box and found a beautiful golden hair slide – the one she had so often admired in the window of the jeweller's shop.

It would have been perfect for binding back her long, shining hair. But now…

'It's lovely,' she said wistfully. 'But surely you could never afford to buy such a precious gift…?'

'I knew how much you wanted it,' he told her, 'so I pawned my gold watch to raise the money. I could never wear it, anyway, because it had such a shabby worn-out strap.'

And Julia gave Jim her little package. He opened it slowly, savouring the surprise. And when he held the fine new strap in his hand, he looked into his wife's eyes and smiled.

'Two lovely gifts,' he said, 'too good to be put to use right away. Let's save them until we can enjoy them properly, and meanwhile, let's enjoy the greatest gift of all – the gift of love.'

Retelling of 'The Gift of the Magi' by O. Henry

86

A Brother's Sacrifice

Back in the fifteenth century, in a tiny village in Germany, there lived a family with eighteen children. Despite a seemingly hopeless situation, two brothers shared a dream to pursue their talent for art. But they knew that the family's financial condition was too tight to pay for their studies.

The two boys came up with their own solution. They would toss a coin. The loser would go into the nearby mines and support his brother attending art academy. Then that brother, at the end of his studies, would support the other brother at the academy, either with sales of his artwork or, if necessary, also by labouring in the mines.

So one brother went to the art academy, while the other went into the dangerous mines. After four years, the young artist returned to his village and family. There was a triumphant homecoming dinner. The artist rose from the table to drink a toast to his beloved brother for his years of sacrifice. His closing words were, 'And now, Albert, it is your turn. Now you can go to the academy to pursue your dream, and I will support you.'

Albert sat there, tears streaming down his face, shaking his lowered head while he sobbed and repeated over and over, 'No... no... no!'

Finally, Albert rose and wiped the tears from his eyes. He looked down the long table, and, holding his hands out in front of him, said softly, 'No, brother, it is too late for me to go. Look... look at what four years in the mines have done to my hands! The bones in every finger have been crushed at least once, and I've been suffering from arthritis so badly that I cannot even hold a wine glass to return your toast, much less make delicate lines on canvas with a pen or brush. No, brother, for me it is too late.'

Then one day, to pay homage to his brother Albert for all that he had sacrificed, Albrecht Dürer painstakingly drew his tortured hands, with palms together and crooked fingers pointing skywards. He called this powerful drawing simply *Hands*, but people soon opened their hearts to the masterpiece and renamed it. They called his tribute of love *The Praying Hands*.

Source unknown

87

The Ragman

I saw a strange sight. I stumbled upon a story most strange, like nothing my life, my street sense, my sly tongue had ever prepared me for. Hush, child. Hush now, and I will tell it to you.

Even before the dawn one Friday morning, I noticed a young man, handsome and strong, walking the alleys of our city. He was pulling an old cart filled with clothes both bright and new, and he was calling in a clear, tenor voice: 'Rags!' Ah, the air was foul and the first light filthy to be crossed by such sweet music.

'Rags! New rags for old! I take your tired rags! Rags!'

'Now, this is a wonder,' I thought to myself, for the man stood tall and his arms were like tree limbs, hard and muscular, and his eyes flashed intelligence. Could he find no better job than this, to be a ragman in the inner city?

I followed him. My curiosity drove me. And I wasn't disappointed. Soon the ragman saw a woman sitting on her back porch. She was sobbing into a handkerchief, sighing and shedding a thousand tears. Her knees and elbows made a sad X. Her shoulders shook. Her heart was breaking.

The ragman stopped his cart. Quietly, he walked to the woman, stepping round tin cans and dead toys.

'Give me your rag,' he said so gently, 'and I'll give you another.'

He slipped the handkerchief from her eyes. She looked up, and he laid across her palm a linen cloth so clean and new that it shone. She blinked from the gift to the giver.

Then, as he began to pull his cart again, the ragman did a strange thing: he put her stained handkerchief to his own face, and then *he* began to weep, to sob as grievously as she had done, his shoulders shaking. Yet she was left without a tear.

'This is a wonder,' I breathed to myself, and I followed the sobbing ragman like a child who cannot turn away from mystery.

'Rags! Rags! New rags for old!' In a little while, when the sky showed grey behind the rooftops and I could see the shredded curtains hanging out of black windows, the ragman came upon a girl whose head was wrapped in a bandage, whose eyes were empty. Blood soaked her bandage. A single line of blood ran down her cheek.

Now the tall ragman looked upon this child with pity, and he drew a lovely yellow bonnet from his cart.

'Give me your rag,' he said, tracing his own line on her cheek, 'and I'll give you mine.'

The child could only gaze at him while he loosened the bandage, removed it, and tied it to his own head. The bonnet he set on hers. And I gasped at what I saw: for with the bandage went the wound! Against his brow it ran a darker, more substantial blood – his own!

'Rags! Rags! I take old rags!' cried the sobbing, bleeding, strong, intelligent ragman.

The sun hurt both the sky, now, and my eyes; the ragman seemed more and more to hurry.

'Are you going to work?' he asked a man who leaned against a telephone pole. The man shook his head.

The ragman pressed him: 'Do you have a job?'

'Are you crazy?' sneered the other. He pulled away from the pole, revealing the right sleeve of his jacket – flat, the cuff stuffed into the pocket. He had no arm.

'So,' said the ragman. 'Give me your jacket, and I'll give you mine.'

Such quiet authority in his voice! The one-armed man took off his jacket. So did the ragman – and I trembled at what I saw: for the ragman's arm stayed in its sleeve, and when the other put it on he had two good arms, thick as tree limbs, but the ragman had only one.

'Go to work,' he said.

After that, he found a drunk, lying unconscious beneath an army blanket, an old man, hunched, wizened and sick. He took that blanket and wrapped it round himself, but for the drunk, he left new clothes.

And now I had to run to keep up with the ragman. Though he was weeping uncontrollably, and bleeding freely at the forehead, pulling his cart with one arm, stumbling for drunkenness, falling again and again, exhausted, old, and sick, yet he went with terrible speed. On spider's legs, he skittered through the alleys of the city, this mile and the next, until he came to its limits, and then he rushed beyond.

I wept to see the change in this man. I hurt to see his sorrow. And yet I needed to see where he was going in such haste, perhaps to know what drove him so.

The little old ragman – he came to a landfill. He came to the garbage pits. And then I wanted to help him in what he did, but I hung back, hiding.

He climbed a hill. With tormented labour, he cleared a little space on that hill. Then he sighed. He lay down. He pillowed his head on a handkerchief and a jacket. He covered his bones with an army blanket. And he died.

Oh, how I cried to witness that death! I slumped in a junked car, and wailed and mourned as one who has no hope – because I had come to love the ragman. Every other face had faded in the wonder of this man, and I cherished him; but he died. I sobbed myself to sleep.

I did not know – how could I know? – that I slept through Friday night and Saturday and its night too.

But then, on Sunday morning, I was wakened by a violence.

Light – pure, hard, demanding light – slammed against my sour face, and I blinked, and I looked, and I saw the last and the first wonder of all. There was the ragman, folding the blanket most carefully, a scar on his forehead, but alive! And besides that – healthy! There was no sign now of age, and all the rags that he had gathered shone with cleanliness.

Well, then I lowered my head and, trembling for all that I had seen, I myself walked up to the ragman. I told him my name with shame, for I was a sorry figure next to him. Then I took off all my clothes in that place, and I said to him with dear yearning in my voice, 'Dress me!'

He dressed me. My Lord, he put new rags on me, and I am a wonder beside him. The ragman, the ragman, the Christ!

Walter Wangerin

The Prince and the Swallow

In the middle of a town, there once stood a monument, erected in honour of a much-loved prince. This monument was covered from head to toe in gold leaf, and his eyes were made from two wonderful sapphires. On his shield was a red ruby.

One day, a little swallow arrived in the town, on her flight south to the warmer climate of Egypt, and she wanted to rest for the night on the prince's shoulder. All at once, the swallow noticed drops of water falling on her feathers. 'How come?' the swallow thought. 'There isn't a cloud to be seen.' She looked all around and up and down, and realized that the prince was weeping!

'Why are you weeping, dear prince? Surely you are wealthy and happy?'

'Oh, little swallow,' the prince replied. 'Now that I can stand here and look down across the city, I can see into every corner, and I am so troubled by the great suffering and need that I see there. Would you help me, little swallow? Just this one night? I am fixed here and I can't move.'

The swallow had a kind heart. 'But only this one night, beautiful prince, because I don't have much time. If I linger too long, the cold weather will catch up with me, and I will die.'

The prince was delighted and thanked the little swallow. 'Thank you,' he said. 'Just be so good as to pick the red ruby out of my shield with your beak, and take it to the mother with the sick child in that little room over there.'

And the swallow picked at the ruby, and eventually had the precious jewel in her beak. She flew in through the open window, and dropped the ruby in the lap of the mother, who had fallen asleep, exhausted.

The next day, the swallow wanted to fly away. But the prince begged her: 'Please, little swallow. Stay one more night! There is an old man, stiff with the cold. Take him my precious blue sapphire. Pick it out of my eye.'

'Oh no, dear prince, I can't pick your eye out,' protested the swallow.

'Please, do as I ask!' So the swallow picked out the sapphire, and eventually freed it, and took it to the poor old man.

On the third evening, the prince begged the swallow again: 'Dear swallow, please stay one more night. A family has arrived from a foreign country. Take my other eye; with this jewel they can rent themselves a place to live.'

But the swallow was unwilling. 'Then you would be blind!'

The prince replied, 'I will see with my heart!'

So the swallow picked at the second sapphire until it was free, and she took the prince's second eye to the immigrant family. When she returned, she said to the prince, 'I won't fly to Egypt now. I will stay with you. You can't see any more, and I can't leave you now.'

During the day, from then on, the swallow would fly round, observing where the need was greatest. Then she would report back to the prince, who would ask her to pick off one of the pieces of gold leaf from his body to help relieve the suffering in the town. One after another, the pieces of gold were picked off and carried away by the swallow to those who were in the most need.

And the strange thing was that the more exposed and poor the prince became, the happier he seemed to be. And the swallow, too, discovered great joy welling up in her own heart.

Then came the cold weather, and she realized that she would soon die. 'Dear prince,' she whispered. 'I will soon have to leave you.'

'Yes, my good and faithful little swallow. You fly off now to Egypt!'

'No, I wouldn't manage that any more,' were her last words to him. And she fell down dead at his feet.

Now that the prince's monument looked so shabby, the people of the town dismantled it and melted it down. Only the prince's heart refused to be destroyed. So the people threw it on the rubbish tip, next to the dead swallow.

'Bring me the two most precious treasures of this town,' said God to his angel. And the angel flew down to the rubbish tip, and brought God the heart of the prince and a little dead swallow.

'You have chosen well,' said God. 'In my kingdom, these will be the closest to me – they gave everything they had for the love of my people.'

Retelling of 'The Happy Prince' by Oscar Wilde

The Boat

There was a young lad who grew up by the seaside. He had a real love of, and fascination with, boats. He got a small block of timber and began to carve a model boat for himself. This boat was going to be perfect, because it would represent everything beautiful that he had ever seen in boats.

When he was finished, he painted it his favourite colour, and he even put his name on it. Then he rigged up tiny sails, and the labour of love was complete.

It would not be a real boat, he thought, unless he put it into the water. So, down to the sea he went and he watched proudly as it bobbed about on the waves. He was so proud of it and so lost in his admiration that it was some time before he realized what was happening. He had given it sails, and the wind was blowing it firmly but gently further and further away from him. He called out to it, as if it should obey him, but it was now under another influence. He watched in horror and great pain as it drifted away out to sea.

He was really upset when he got home, and he didn't sleep too well that night. Then, one day, he was passing a toy shop and was jolted out of his depression by the sight of a toy boat in the window – and yes, it was his boat! He rushed in eagerly to claim it, but the shopkeeper coldly dismissed his claims, saying that it belonged to him now, and if the boy wanted it, he would have to buy it.

The boy rushed home and told his dad. He wanted to know how much he should pay for it, and the father replied, 'If you really need to get the boat, you will have to give everything you have to get it.'

So the boy emptied out all his savings boxes, and ran down to the shop with every penny he had. He placed the money on the counter without even checking it, and rushed back out of the door with his beloved boat. He rubbed it, hugged it, and ran to show it to his dad. 'Ah!' said his dad. 'So this boat is yours now.'

'It surely is mine!' said the boy. 'I made it, and then I bought it back and gave all I had to get it. It's mine indeed – only now it's mine twice over!'

Source unknown

90

The Rolling Coin

A wise old man once owned a precious golden coin. One day, as he sat gazing at this precious coin and rejoicing in its beauty, a thought occurred to him: 'It isn't right that I should be the only person to have the pleasure of possessing this golden coin. What use is it if no one shares it?' And he went out and gave the coin to a passing child.

The child couldn't believe her luck. She couldn't take her eyes off this shining coin. Then she had a sudden idea: 'I'll give this coin to Mum. She needs so many things. This coin will make her very happy.'

Of course, the child's mother was delighted with the coin – such an unexpected solution to so many of her problems. She pondered in her mind as to how to spend it and what to buy first.

As she was thinking about this there was a knock at the door, and there stood a street beggar. 'Poor soul,' she thought. 'He has nothing, and we are just about getting by.' And she gave the gold coin to the beggar.

The beggar was speechless. This coin could be turned into food for a month. He made his way back to the subway where he slept, and there he noticed a new resident, just arrived. The poor guy was blind and disabled. No chance of getting anywhere near to the folks who might have spared him a coin or two.

'I guess he needs it more than I do,' he thought to himself. And he pressed the gold coin into the blind man's thin, cold fingers.

That evening, the wise old man walked through the dark subway. He noticed the blind, disabled beggar and stopped to speak to him. The beggar couldn't remember the last time anyone had bothered to speak to him.

After a while, the wise old man put his arm round the beggar's shoulder. 'I've nothing left to give you, except my friendship,' he murmured.

A tear rolled across the cheek of the blind beggar. How could he ever repay this gift of human kindness that had changed a dark night into a new dawn? With his shaking, aching hands, he reached into his pocket, brought out the golden coin and gave it to his new-found friend.

'Thank you for loving me,' he said.

Source unknown

91

Cooperation

One morning, the sun got up in a bad mood. 'I'm really tired of getting up every morning and giving light to the earth, day after day,' it said. 'I'm tired of ripening the corn and melting the snow. What does the human race ever do for me in return?'

The sun was still thinking all this over, when the rain arrived.

'Lady Rain,' the sun remarked, 'you water the earth all the time and make the flowers grow. You turn the fields green, and fill up the rivers. What does the human race ever do for you in return?'

Hearing this, the rain furrowed her brow, broke out in a terrible noise and fell headlong onto the earth. And as she fell, she pounded out these words: 'Listen, Mother Earth. You let humankind work you, rip you open, scratch and scrape you. What does the human race ever do for you in return?'

The earth turned into its own furrows and murmured to the grain of wheat, 'Hey, little grain of wheat. You let yourself die so that humankind can eat bread. What does the human race ever do for you in return?'

And then the sun stopped shining.

The rain stopped falling.

The earth stopped holding the grain.

The grain stopped germinating.

And life disappeared from the face of the earth.

Eventually, the sun became bored, because there were no longer any children dancing in its warmth and light.

The rain became saddened at never seeing the smile of the gardener in his garden.

The earth became weary at never hearing the joyful steps of the labourer on her back.

And the grain of wheat began to rot in solitude.

Together, they decided to have a meeting with God, the creator, and this is what they said to him: 'Lord, everything is dying in this universe that you created to be so good and fruitful. Give back life to the earth, we beg you.'

And God replied, 'My friends, I have given you everything you need to support life on earth. Life cannot be born except of you and between you. And life will be born anew if each of you shares of its nature with all creation. For life is born out of a sharing of life. And where cooperation is refused, life cannot be.'

Retelling of a French parable

The Map

Once, a father was looking after his children and trying to keep them entertained, but he wasn't having too much success. It was a wet Saturday, and the children were getting bored. They were starting to get on his nerves, with their restlessness and their constant chattering.

But the man was inventive, and suddenly he had an idea. He took down a magazine from the shelf and opened it up, looking through it until he found a map of the world printed on one page. He tore this page out of the magazine, and proceeded to cut it up with scissors into small pieces. Then he jumbled up all the pieces and placed them in a pile on the floor, like the pieces of a jigsaw.

Then he set his two young sons the task of putting the map together again, thinking that this would keep them quiet for a good long time. He left them with it and went off to make himself a cup of coffee.

Imagine his amazement, therefore, when five minutes later he came back to find the map neatly and accurately put back together again.

'How did you manage to put it back together again so quickly?' he asked them, taken aback by their skill.

'Oh, it was easy,' the younger boy replied. 'You told us it was a map of the world, and when we looked at the pieces, at first we didn't know where to begin to sort it all out. It seemed impossible. But then we realized that there was a picture of a man on the other side, so we just put the man back together again. When we turned it over, the world had come back together again as well!'

'Yes, Dad,' chimed in the other brother. 'It's ever so easy. If you put the man right, the world is OK.'

Source unknown

The Mustard Seed

The old couple who lived in a cottage on the edge of the village were envied for the happiness of their marriage. They never quarrelled and were always affectionate to one another. Sadly, after thirty-four years of this happiness, the husband became ill and died.

The wife was overcome with grief. Her children tried to console her, but to no avail. Her neighbours tried to console her, but with similar lack of success. Weeks and months went by, and still the woman was grieving; tears fell down her cheeks from morning until night.

Then a holy man came to the village. People told him about the woman, and asked him to try to help her. The holy man went to the woman's house. Dressed in his rough woollen tunic, he sat down with the grieving widow and listened carefully to her story. When she had spilled out all her sorrow, he reached into one of the deep pockets in his tunic, and drew out a tiny little mustard seed. 'I think I may have a cure for your grief,' he said. 'I want you to go round the people in this region, and look for a family that has no sorrows. When you find this family, give them this little mustard seed, and then come back to me.'

The woman set off in search of such a family. She visited every home in the district, and talked to the people. She listened to their stories, just as the holy man had listened to hers. In time, she almost forgot about the mustard seed, because every single family she met was carrying some kind of sorrow.

One day, she happened to meet the holy man again, and he stopped to ask how she was feeling. She was surprised at first, by his question, then she suddenly remembered the mustard seed, still safely in her purse.

'I'm so sorry. I haven't found a family without sorrows yet,' she told him.

'But you yourself are cured of your grief,' he smiled. 'The mustard seed is a great healer!'

Source unknown

Our
Relationship
with All
Creation

94

The Agreement

Once upon a time, before there were any people walking around in this valley, there were bears. They had an agreement with the salmon.

The salmon would come upriver every autumn, and the bears would acknowledge this and take what they needed. This is the way it was with everything. Everyone lived by certain agreements and courtesies. But the salmon and the bears had made no agreement with the river. It had been overlooked. No one thought it was even necessary.

Well, it was. One autumn, the river pulled itself back into the shore trees and wouldn't let the salmon enter from the ocean. Whenever they tried, the river would pull back and leave the salmon stranded on the beach. There was a long argument, a lot of talk. Finally, the river let the salmon enter. But when the salmon got up into this country where the bears lived, the river began to run in two directions at once, north on one side, south on the other, roaring, heaving white water and rolling big boulders up on the banks. Then the river was suddenly still. The salmon were afraid to move. The bears were standing behind trees, looking out. The river said in the middle of all this silence that there had to be an agreement. No one could just do something, whatever they wanted. You couldn't just take someone for granted.

So for several days, they spoke about it. The salmon said who they were and where they came from, and the bears spoke about what they did, what powers they had been given, and the river spoke about its agreement with the rain and the wind and the crayfish and so on. Everybody said what they needed and what they would give away. Then a very odd thing happened – the river said it loved the salmon. No one had ever said anything like this before. No one had taken this chance. It was an honesty that pleased everyone. It made for a very deep agreement among them.

Well, they were able to reach an understanding about their obligations to each other, and everyone went his way. This remains unchanged. Time has nothing to do with this. This is not a story. When you feel the river shuddering against your legs, you are feeling the presence of all these agreements.

Barry Lopez

95

The Broken Arc

A man lived in an old stone cottage that was badly in need of repair. He made do, day by day, and got on with his life, struggling to wrench a living from the meagre land. But eventually, the rain that leaked in on him got too heavy, and the wind around his ears got too cold. He had to do something about the gap in his wall.

Up on the hillside, there stood an ancient stone Celtic cross. It had stood there since time immemorial. It was silent and uncomplaining in the Atlantic gales that swept over it, but its very silence said something about continuity, community and interrelatedness. It had become part of the local imagination, and without ever really thinking about it, the people knew with a sound instinct that it was important. It had something to say about what they hoped to be. Something to do with the coming of the kingdom.

The cottager went up to the cross one dark night. One of those stone arcs, he thought, would exactly fit the hole in his wall. He would come the next day with a hammer and chisel, and chip it away. He smiled, perhaps uneasily, as he thought of how much warmer his home would be without the perpetual draughts. Almost satisfied with his decision, he turned back towards his homeward path, but his plans were rudely interrupted. In the distance he clearly saw flames rising from his cottage. Panic-stricken, he ran home across the rough fields. But when he arrived, his home was still standing as he had left it. The fire had only been in his imagination.

Common sense reasserted itself, and a few days later, he set off up the hill again with his hammer and chisel. It was dark, but he looked around warily, lest anyone should see him there. It was only a piece of stone, after all, and he needed it. He started to chip. The sound of his hammer against the solid head of the chisel rang out through the night like the tolling of a bell, to alarm the very heavens. But he carried on chipping, until he remembered the strange events of his previous visit and looked over his shoulder nervously in the direction of his cottage. And there, on the distant skyline, a fire raged. And again, he ran home in terror. And again, he found his cottage unharmed, just as he had left it.

More cold, damp nights came and went. Sleep came uneasily. The bizarre images of dream and nightmare entangled themselves among the pressing urgencies of every day. The fierce winds from the sea were stronger by far than the breezes that fluttered through his unease. He made up his mind that, the very next day, his cottage would be sound again, and that no irrational fears would deflect him from his purpose.

He walked up the hill, without looking to right or left. He worked quickly and efficiently. He closed the doors of his mind firmly against any distraction, real or imagined. Soon, the stone arc was in his sack. This time, there were no flames on the horizon, and no flash of panic disturbed him. He turned his back on the mutilated cross and walked home steadily, through the quiet of the night. And when he got home, the cottage was a heap of smouldering ashes.

Retelling of an Irish folk story

96

The Perfect Globe

In a museum, many ages ago, there was an amazing exhibit. It was a tiny globe, just a few feet in diameter, yet it held so much mystery and so much beauty within it that people travelled for miles and miles, just to see it. There were always crowds around it, and queues lined up, patiently waiting for their turn to view the wonder.

And there it was – a delicate sphere floating in its case. It looked different from every angle. Sometimes, you could see big pools of water in it, and smaller flows of water feeding into the big pools. Sometimes, these pools were smooth and blue, and at other times, they were white with froth and full of movement. There were bumps on the globe – some big bumps, with white tops, and some smaller, gentler bumps. You could have run your fingers over the bumps, feeling the sharp spikes on some of them, and the velvety textures of the others. The globe had little sandpits in it, with lovely patterns blown by the wind, which changed every day, and it had frosty places too, which burned your fingers with the cold if you touched them. And it danced in the space around it, turning on its toes, so every part of it got a turn at facing the light and at resting in the darkness.

People marvelled at the thin layer of gas that surrounded this little globe, and noticed that there were holes in it, and that these holes seemed to be getting bigger. They were concerned, in case something was going wrong with it. And sometimes, parts of it would go dark for no apparent reason, and there might be smoke and a strange smell from those parts, and the people didn't know why, and they were concerned, because these dark bits never quite seemed to get better again afterwards.

Perhaps most of all, though, people gasped in wonder at the tiny creatures that lived on the globe. Some lived in the pools, and some lived just under the gas wrapping, and others lived on the bumps.

The globe was declared a national treasure, and people paid large sums of money to make sure that it was protected. It had become so precious to them that they would have defended it with their own lives. They would never let anyone hurt it. It came to be known as the greatest wonder of all time, and people flocked to see it, to touch it and to love it. They felt that just to be in touch with it would bring them healing, and just to gaze at it deeply would bring them wisdom. They even felt that, without it, their own lives would be meaningless.

That was all a long time ago. The treasure has fallen into disrepair now. Some say that the rot set in when the people who used to treasure the globe started to shrivel and shrink because they were so wrapped up in less important matters. The people eventually got so small that they disappeared right inside the globe, and after that, they never noticed it again, and they completely forgot how they had once treasured and loved it. With no one to cherish it, the globe slowly stopped breathing, and eventually it slipped away into space, unregarded.

Retelling of a traditional story

97

The Soup Stone

A woman in a village was surprised to find a fairly well-dressed stranger at her door, asking for something to eat. 'I'm sorry,' she said. 'I have nothing in the house right now.'

'Not to worry,' said the amiable stranger. 'I have a soup stone in this satchel of mine; if you will let me put it in a pot of boiling water, I'll make the most delicious soup in the world. A very large pot, please.'

The woman was curious. She put the pot on the fire and whispered the secret of the soup stone to a neighbour. By the time the water began to boil, all the neighbours had gathered to see the stranger and his soup stone. The stranger dropped the stone into the water, then tasted a teaspoonful with relish and exclaimed, 'Ah, delicious! All it needs is some potatoes.'

'I have potatoes in my kitchen,' shouted one woman. In a few minutes, she was back with a large quantity of sliced potatoes, which were thrown into the pot.

Then the stranger tasted the brew again. 'Excellent!' he said, but added wistfully, 'If we only had some meat, this would become a tasty stew.'

Another housewife rushed home to bring some meat, which the stranger accepted graciously and flung into the pot. When he tasted the broth again, he rolled his eyes heavenwards and said, 'Ah, tasty! If we had some vegetables, it would be perfect, absolutely perfect.'

One of the neighbours rushed off home, and returned with a basketful of carrots and onions. After these had been thrown in too, and the stranger had tasted the mixture, he said in a voice of command, 'Salt and sauce.'

'Right here,' said the housewife.

Then came another command: 'Bowls for everyone.' People rushed to their homes in search of bowls. Some even brought back bread and fruit.

Then they all sat down to a delicious meal while the stranger handed out large helpings of his incredible soup. Everyone felt strangely happy as they laughed and talked and shared their very first common meal. In the middle of the merriment, the stranger quietly slipped away, leaving behind the miraculous soup stone, which they could use any time they wanted to make the loveliest soup in the world.

Anthony de Mello

98

Monkeys, Frogs and Badgers

There were once three big, bare mountains. They lived a quiet life. Every day they stood still under the sun. Every night they stood still under the moon.

Then one day, each of them received a catalogue from the postman. The mountains eagerly looked through their catalogues. The first mountain came to the 'monkeys' section, and thought they looked wonderful, so he ordered some of them.

The second mountain was drawn to the 'frogs' section. They looked really marvellous. He immediately ordered some of them.

The third mountain opened his catalogue at the 'badgers' section. He looked no further. Badgers would be perfect.

Night came, but the mountains were so excited that it took them a long time to fall asleep. As they slept, they dreamed of monkeys, frogs and badgers.

Early the next morning, the first mountain woke up to find, at his feet, the monkeys he had ordered. The second mountain looked down and saw all the frogs. The third mountain woke up to find his badgers. All day, the mountains played with their new animals and the new animals enjoyed their new mountains.

But soon, all the animals became hungry, and there was no food. Then the sun went down and there was nowhere for them to go to keep warm, so they lay down on the ground and shivered. Everyone was hungry and uncomfortable. The monkeys wished there was a light, because they liked to read at night.

When all the animals had gone to sleep, the mountains had a meeting. They felt terrible. They had only thought of how much fun it would be for them to have the animals. They had never even considered whether the animals would like their new home or not. They realized how selfish they had been.

'We must do everything we can, so that the animals won't leave us,' said the first mountain.

'No, we must do it because it's our duty to take care of them,' said the second mountain.

'We will be good to them because we love them,' said the third mountain.

And so they got out their catalogues.

The next day, there was a big box of food at the foot of each mountain. After a hearty breakfast, the animals felt so good that they sang to the mountains until lunchtime.

In the afternoon, there were more surprises! There were torches for the monkeys, made of starlight, and bouncy balls for the frogs, made from the pebbles that flew across the mountainside, and for the badgers, there were tapes of their favourite dancing tunes, put together by the wind.

When night came, it was cold again. But the mountains had a plan. They told the animals to curl up together in a cosy pile, then they stood over them, making a warm shelter for them.

The animals slept soundly, except for one of the badgers. He came out to yawn at the moon. He noticed that the mountains were shivering with cold.

'Our mountain friends shouldn't suffer to keep us warm,' he said to himself. Then he opened one of the catalogues. He knew just what to order.

The next day, three great big blankets arrived, beautifully decorated with grasses and flowers and shrubs.

That night, when the cold crept up, the animals wrapped the blankets around the mountains. Everyone was comfortable and warm, and everyone slept well. And even when winter came, everyone was happy.

Source unknown

99

Three Sabbaths

In a small village, three friends – a Muslim, a Jew and a Christian – farmed on adjoining land. The Muslim observed Friday as the Sabbath, the Jew observed Saturday as the Sabbath and the Christian observed Sunday as the Sabbath.

One autumn Friday, around noon, the Jew and the Christian finished ploughing their fields. As he sat eating his lunch, the Christian noticed that the field of his Muslim friend was not yet ploughed. 'If he does not plough it today, it may rain tomorrow and he will not be able to complete his planting. I could plough a bit of his field and thus make his work easier.' And he did.

In an adjoining field, his Jewish companion came upon an identical plan. Without consulting each other, the two men completed their neighbour's ploughing.

The next day, when the Muslim discovered that his field had been ploughed, he rejoiced saying, 'Surely, God has sent his angels to plough my field while I observed his day of rest.'

Months later, when harvest season arrived, the fields of the three friends flourished. One Sunday, the Jew and the Muslim were harvesting their crop while their Christian brother celebrated the Sabbath. As he completed harvesting his corn, the Jew noticed that the field of his Christian friend was ready to harvest. 'If he does not harvest today, he could lose a part of his crop,' he thought. 'I will pick his corn until it becomes dark.' And he did.

Completely unknown to him, his Muslim brother came to the same conclusion. Between them, they harvested their friend's entire field.

On Monday, when the Christian came out to the field, he discovered that his entire crop had been harvested. 'It is a miracle,' he thought. 'While I rested, God's angels harvested.'

During threshing season, the Muslim and the Christian were working on a Saturday, while their Jewish friend stayed at home, keeping the Sabbath holy. As he finished threshing his grain, the Muslim looked to the next field and thought, 'If my Jewish neighbour does not gather his grain today, the rain might wash it away and he will lose his crop. I will thresh part of his crop this afternoon.' And he did.

Unknown to him, his Christian friend decided upon the same course of action. Separately, the two men threshed, bound and covered the entire crop.

When his Sabbath was over, the Jewish farmer discovered that his grain was threshed. Lifting his eyes to heaven he prayed, 'Blessed are you, Lord of the universe, for sending your angels while I was keeping your Sabbath.'

William White

100

The Great Hooray

The children of Classes 1 and 2 were assembled in the hall, waiting for the class to begin. The visiting poet was with them this morning, and they were all agog with excitement. They always enjoyed his visits. But Class 3 was late. The children were getting impatient.

The poet looked around at their eager faces. An unnatural quiet descended, as they seemed almost to be holding their breath in anticipation.

'You're so quiet today,' he smiled at them. 'Let's see if you can make a noise! Let's all shout "Hooray!".'

So a shout went up: 'Hooray!'

'That's splendid,' he beamed. 'Now, when Class 3 arrives, let's play a game with them. Let's all be as quiet as mice. And when they are all in their places, we'll all shout a huge "Hooray!" to greet them. We'll see if we can raise the roof! Agreed?'

The children were thrilled at the idea. They became quiet again, and you could have heard a pin drop. Class 3 came into the hall. They were sorry they were late. They sat down quietly. And then, on a signal from the poet…

'Hooray!'

The great Hooray resounded through the hall, through the school, through the whole village. And – oh! Imagine! The roof flew off!

Off it flew, leaving the blue sky open above the children's heads. Off it flew over the gardens and houses, the streets and the trees. And as it went, it dropped 'hoorays' off all over the town. Mums doing the washing up suddenly found a 'hooray' in the kitchen. Dogs fast asleep in their corners were awoken by the happy sounds trickling down from the sky as the roof flew past.

Through keyholes, windows and open doors the hoorays crept into every home. Whispers and echoes of joy covered the whole community with morning mystery. Hearts fluttered and lifted at the happy sound.

And the roof flew on and on, carrying echoes of joy through the world, and bringing the rafters of homes throughout the land into resonance. Later, in the night, the rain came, and every raindrop picked up the sound of the great hooray. The next morning, the mist that covered the hills and valleys was impregnated with the same cry of joy. It trickled away into the streams and rivers. It crept up the stalk of every flower and nestled in the feathers of every bird.

Hooray, hooray, hooray!

As the weeks passed by, the gentle waves lapped against a distant seashore, and the close-curled shells, if you listened closely, recalled that first hooray.

Years later, the poet smiled, as the echoes of the first hooray gently touched his face again in a passing breeze. He knew another poet. The poet whose first joyous hooray had soaked into everything that is. He knew that his own poems were a tiny echo of that great poem of creation, and he laughed out loud at the mystery of it all. And his laughter bubbled off and away, to gurgle forever through the universe.

Retelling of 'Hooray' by Ted Walter

Acknowledgments

Wisdom stories live in the atmosphere we breathe. They have a life of their own, and they evolve and change with every retelling. In many cases, it is impossible to identify their origins, and most of the stories in this collection have been gleaned over the years from oral retellings. Whenever the source of a story is known, it is detailed in this Acknowledgments section and referred to briefly beneath the story itself. Every effort has been made to trace and contact copyright owners for material used in this book. We apologize for any inadvertent omissions or errors.

1. Retelling by Margaret Silf of a traditional story.
2. Abridged from *The Tale of Geronimo Grub* retold by Pat Wynnejones, published by Lion Publishing, 1991, 2000, copyright © 1990 Pat Wynnejones.
3. Retelling by Margaret Silf of a traditional story, incorporating text from *Wayfaring* by Margaret Silf, published by Darton, Longman and Todd, 2001.
4. Retelling by Margaret Silf of a traditional story.
5. Retelling by Margaret Silf of a story from *The Song of the Bird* by Anthony de Mello, copyright © 1982 Anthony de Mello, SJ. Used by permission of Doubleday, a division of Random House, Inc., and The Center for Spiritual Exchange.
6. Extract from *The Velveteen Rabbit* by Margery Williams, copyright © 1922 The Estate of Margery Williams, published by Egmont Books Limited, London, and used with permission.
7. Retelling by Margaret Silf of a Swedish legend.
8. Retelling by Margaret Silf of a traditional story.
9. Story from *Heart of the Enlightened* by Anthony de Mello, copyright

© 1989 by The Center for Spiritual Exchange. Used by permission of Doubleday, a division of Random House, Inc., and The Center for Spiritual Exchange.

10. Source unknown.

11. Story by Margaret Silf.

12. Retelling by Margaret Silf of a traditional story.

13. Story by Amy le Feuvre.

14. Retelling by Margaret Silf of a traditional story.

15. Story from *Celtic Parables* by Robert van de Weyer, published by SPCK, 1997. Used by permission.

16. Source unknown.

17. Retelling by Margaret Silf of a traditional story.

18. Source unknown.

19. Retelling by Margaret Silf of a traditional East European story.

20. Source unknown.

21. Source unknown.

22. Retelling by Margaret Silf of a traditional story.

23. Source unknown.

24. Source unknown.

25. Source unknown.

26. Source unknown.

27. Story from *Invitations* by Francis Dewar, published by SPCK, 1996. Used by permission.

28. Retelling by Margaret Silf of a story by Hans Christian Andersen.

29. Source unknown.

30. Source unknown.

31. Retelling by Margaret Silf of a Northumbrian community story.

32. Source unknown.

33. Story from *Tales of a Magic Monastery* by Theophane the Monk, published by The Crossroad Publishing Company, New York, 1996.

34. Retelling by Anthony Nanson of a story heard from the English storyteller Richard Walker, who in turn heard it from the American storyteller Dan Keding, who shaped the story around a saying he was told by his Serbian mother.

35. Based on an incident reported in the 1930s by James N.

McCutcheon from a New York courtroom while Fiorello LaGuardia was mayor of the city.

36. Source unknown.

37. Source unknown.

38. Retelling by Margaret Silf of a traditional Mediterranean story.

39. Source unknown.

40. Source unknown.

41. Retelling by Margaret Silf of a traditional story.

42. Retelling by Margaret Silf of a traditional Indian story.

43. Source unknown.

44. Retelling by Margaret Silf of a traditional Philippine story.

45. 'The Water of Life', copyright © Kate Compston, from *Wisdom is Calling*, compiled by Geoffrey Duncan, published by The Canterbury Press. Used by permission.

46. Retelling by Margaret Silf of a traditional story.

47. Retelling by Margaret Silf of a traditional story.

48. Retelling by Margaret Silf of a traditional story.

49. Story from *Heart of the Enlightened* by Anthony de Mello, copyright © 1989 by The Center for Spiritual Exchange. Used by permission of Doubleday, a division of Random House, Inc., and The Center for Spiritual Exchange.

50. Retelling by Margaret Silf of a Chinese folk story.

51. Source unknown.

52. Retelling by Margaret Silf of a traditional Indian story.

53. Retelling by Margaret Silf of a story by Leo Tolstoy.

54. Retelling by Margaret Silf of a traditional story.

55. Retelling by Margaret Silf of a story by Fyodor Dostoevsky from *The Brothers Karamazov*.

56. Retelling by Margaret Silf of a Jewish folk story.

57. Retelling by Margaret Silf of an Armenian folk story.

58. Source unknown.

59. Retelling by Margaret Silf of a West African fable from *The Hero with a Thousand Faces* by Joseph Campbell, published by Princeton Press, 1949.

60. Source unknown.

61. Retelling by Margaret Silf of a traditional Franciscan story, based on 'The Wolf of Gubbio'.

62. Retelling by Margaret Silf of an Arabian fable.

63. Retelling by Margaret Silf of a traditional story.

64. Source unknown.

65. Retelling by Margaret Silf of a Jewish folk story.

66. Story from *The Alchemist* by Paulo Coelho, translated by Alan R. Clarke, published by HarperCollins, London, and HarperCollins Publishers, Inc., New York. Copyright © 1988 by Paulo Coelho. English translation copyright © 1993 by Paulo Coelho and Alan R. Clarke. Reprinted by permission of HarperCollins Publishers Ltd and HarperCollins Publishers, Inc.

67. Source unknown.

68. Source unknown.

69. Source unknown.

70. Retelling by Margaret Silf of a story by Leo Tolstoy.

71. Story from *The Legend of the Bells and Other Tales* by John Shea, published by ACTA Publications, Chicago, 1996.

72. Story by Aesop.

73. Source unknown.

74. Source unknown.

75. Story from *The Alchemist* by Paulo Coelho, translated by Alan R. Clarke, published by HarperCollins, London, and HarperCollins Publishers, Inc., New York. Copyright © 1988 by Paulo Coelho. English translation copyright © 1993 by Paulo Coelho and Alan R. Clarke. Reprinted by permission of HarperCollins Publishers Ltd and HarperCollins Publishers, Inc.

76. Retelling by Margaret Silf of a traditional story.

77. Source unknown.

78. Story from *Heart of the Enlightened* by Anthony de Mello, copyright © 1989 by The Center for Spiritual Exchange. Used by permission of Doubleday, a division of Random House, Inc., and The Center for Spiritual Exchange.

79. Retelling by Margaret Silf of a traditional oriental story.

80. Retelling by Anthony Nanson of a story heard from the English

storyteller Helen East, who found it among the Bushman tales recorded by Laurens van der Post in *The Heart of the Hunter*.

81. Retelling by Margaret Silf of a traditional story.

82. Retelling by Margaret Silf of a traditional German story.

83. Source unknown.

84. Retelling by Margaret Silf of a Comanche legend.

85. Retelling by Margaret Silf of 'The Gift of the Magi' by O. Henry (William Sydney Porter).

86. Source unknown.

87. Story from *Ragman and Other Cries of Faith* by Walter Wangerin, copyright © 1984 Walter Wangerin Jnr, published by HarperCollins, San Francisco.

88. Retelling by Margaret Silf of 'The Happy Prince' by Oscar Wilde.

89. Source unknown.

90. Source unknown.

91. Retelling by Margaret Silf of a French parable.

92. Source unknown.

93. Source unknown.

94. Story from *Desert Notes and River Notes* by Barry Lopez, published by Picador, 1990.

95. Retelling by Margaret Silf of an Irish folk story.

96. Retelling by Margaret Silf of a traditional story.

97. Story from *Heart of the Enlightened* by Anthony de Mello, copyright © 1989 by The Center for Spiritual Exchange. Used by permission of Doubleday, a division of Random House, Inc., and The Center for Spiritual Exchange.

98. Source unknown.

99. Story from *Stories for the Journey* by William R. White, copyright © 1988 Augsburg Publishing House. Used by permission of Augsburg Fortress.

100. Prose retelling of 'Hooray', a poem by Ted Walter, from *Little Book of Poems*, Forward Press Ltd, Peterborough.

ALSO FROM LION PUBLISHING:

The Way of Wisdom

By Margaret Silf

As we survey our lives, many of us feel that we may be missing out on something deeper and more important. Isn't there more to life than this? Where do we come from? How can we connect more deeply with the world around us? Where can we find a guiding wisdom?

Margaret Silf draws on wisdom from around the world and across the ages to respond to questions such as these. Blending her own text with a rich array of quotations from sources such as new science and cosmology, folk stories, natural history, poetry, and scripture, she covers seven main themes: original wisdom, indigenous wisdom, natural wisdom, life wisdom, desert wisdom, guiding wisdom, and unfolding wisdom.

The Way of Wisdom will appeal to all those searching for a deeper meaning and sense of connectedness in their lives.

ISBN 978 0 7459 5210 9

Soul Searchers

An anthology of spiritual journeys

Compiled by Teresa de Bertodano

From the beginning of human history, men and women have travelled the earth. This collection of stories describes the journeying of the human spirit. The stories span four millennia and five continents, and they resonate with the deepest yearnings of the human soul.

The book is divided into three sections or Journeys. The first Journey takes us through the challenging childhood and teenage years. The second Journey happens when all previous certainties are questioned, which can occur at any time from our twenties to our fifties. The third Journey takes us into the final stage of life, when we are moving towards death.

This book is for all those interested in the journey of the human spirit. It is a beautiful and wide-ranging compilation that will delight and inspire.

ISBN 978 0 7459 5041 9